Sincere

warm regards

[signature]

You Can Change the World

THE GLOBAL CITIZEN'S HANDBOOK FOR LIVING ON PLANET EARTH

‿

A Report of the Club of Budapest

Ervin Laszlo

Introduction By
Mikhail Gorbachev

Postscript By
Paulo Coelho

Contribution By
Masami Saionji

SelectBooks, Inc.

You Can Change the World
© 2003 by Ervin Laszlo.
All rights reserved.

Masami Saionji's contributions to this book have been adapted from
Vision for the 21st Century (publication pending) and *You Are the Universe* (2001),
© 2003 by Masami Saionji.

This edition published by SelectBooks, Inc. For information address
SelectBooks, Inc., New York, New York.

All rights reserved. Published in the United States of America.
No part of this book may be used or reproduced in any manner
whatsoever without the written permission of the publisher.

First Edition

ISBN 1-59079-057-X

Library of Congress Cataloging-in-Publication Data

Laszlo, Ervin, 1932-
   You can change the world : the global citizen's handbook for living on
planet Earth : a report of the Club of Budapest / by Ervin Laszlo ; with
an introduction by Mikhail Gorbachev ; postscript by Paulo Coelho ;
and a contribution by Masami Saionji.-- 1st ed.
   p. cm.
Includes bibliographical references.
ISBN 1-59079-057-X (alk. paper)
   1. Environmentalism.   2. Environmental responsibility.
I. Club of Budapest.   II. Title.
GE195 .L384 2003
363.7--dc22
                                   2003016789

Illustration on p. 43 by David Palukaitis

Manufactured in the United States of America

10 9 8 7 6 5 4 3 2 1

ॐ ACKNOWLEDGMENTS

I take this opportunity to express my heartfelt thanks to friends and colleagues who have contributed to bringing together the ideas and materials put forward in this Handbook. This means first of all my friends at the Club of Budapest: in particular General Secretary Peter Spiegel of the international secretariat, Germany; Maria Sági and Ivan Vitányi at the Budapest headquarters, Hungary; Nitamo Montecucco, Aleandro Tommasi, and Olivero Beha of the Club of Budapest Italy. My friends of the Club of Budapest USA and North America deserve special thanks: Vinod Kumar Bhalla, Muriel Adcock, Carl Zaiss, and Suheil Bushrui. I am grateful to Honorary Members Mikhail Gorbachev, Masami Saionji and Paulo Coelho for wonderful writings that bring clarity as well as authority to the message I wished to convey. My editors, Jane Taylor of Positive News in England and Daniel Panner of SelectBooks in the U.S., have made excellent suggestions for improving the quality and clarity of the text and helped me complete it with relevant information. Last but not least, I am pleased to acknowledge the dedication, commitment, and expertise of Bill Gladstone of Waterside Productions and Kenzi Sugihara of SelectBooks in bringing out the present edition and making it available in North America and elsewhere in the English-speaking world.

∽CONTENTS

ᘓ THE CLUB OF BUDAPEST

The Club of Budapest, founded in 1993 by Ervin Laszlo, is an informal association of globally and locally active opinion leaders in the fields of art, science, religion, and culture. It is dedicated to furthering and facilitating the evolution of more responsible and timely values and ethics among people in all societies and every walk of life, as the best and ultimately only dependable avenue toward peace and sustainability on this planet. The Club has headquarters in Budapest, an international secretariat in Stuttgart, a coordinating center in Washington, and national Chapters in the USA, Canada, Mexico, Brazil, France, Germany, Italy, Austria, Hungary, India, Japan, China, and Samoa.

Honorary President, Sir Peter Ustinov
Bursins, Switzerland

Founder–President, Prof. Ervin Laszlo
Budapest, Hungary and Montescudaio, Italy

Global Ambassador, Lady Fiona Montagu
Beaulieu, England

General Secretary, Peter Spiegel
Stuttgart, Germany

www.club-of-budapest.org

THE CLUB OF BUDAPEST

❧

INTERNATIONAL
HONORARY MEMBERS

Dsingis **Aitmatov**
Writer

Oscar **Arias**
*Statesman, Nobel Peace
Laureate*

A.T. **Ariyaratne**
Buddhist Spiritual Leader

Maurice **Béjart**
Dancer/Choreographer

Thomas **Berry**
Theologian/Scientist

Karlheinz **Böhm**
Actor/Activist

Sir Arthur C. **Clarke**
Writer

Paulo **Coelho**
Writer

The XIVth **Dalai Lama**
*Spiritual Leader/
Nobel Peace Laureate*

Riane **Eisler**
Feminist Historian/Activist

Milos **Forman**
Film Director

Peter **Gabriel**
Musician

Jane **Goodall**
Scientist

Rivka **Golani**
Musician

Mikhail **Gorbachev**
Opinion Leader/Statesman

Arpád **Göncz**
Writer/Statesman

Otto Herbert **Hajek**
Sculptor

Václav **Havel**
Writer/Statesman

Hazel **Henderson**
Economist/Activist

Pir Vilayat **Inayat-Khan**
Sufi Spiritual Leader

Miklós **Jancsó**
Film Director

Ken-Ichiro **Kobayashi**
Orchestra Director

Gidon **Kremer**
Musician

Hans **Küng**
Christian Spiritual Leader

Shu-hsien **Liu**
Philosopher

Eva **Marton**
Opera Singer

Zubin **Mehta**
Orchestra Director

Edgar **Mitchell**
Scientist/Astronaut

Edgar **Morin**
Philosopher/Sociologist

Robert **Muller**
Educator/Activist

Ute-Henriette **Ohoven**
Unesco Ambassador

Gillo **Pontecorvo**
Film Director

Mary **Robinson**
*Political and Human
Rights Leader*

Mstislav **Rostropovich**
Orchestra Director

Sir Joseph **Rotblat**
Scientist/Nobel Peace Laureate

Peter **Russell**
Philosopher/Futurist

Masami **Saionji**
Japanese Spiritual Leader

Karan **Singh**
Hindu Spiritual Leader

Sir Sigmund **Sternberg**
Interfaith Spiritual Leader

Archbishop Desmond **Tutu**
*Spiritual Leader/Nobel
Peace Laureate*

Liv **Ullmann**
Actor/Director

Sir Peter **Ustinov**
Actor/Writer/Director

Vigdis **Finnbogadottir**
Political Leader

Richard von **Weizsäcker**
Opinion Leader/Statesman

Elie **Wiesel**
Writer/Nobel Peace Laureate

Betty **Williams**
Activist/Nobel Peace Laureate

Mohammed **Yunus**
Economist/Activist

INTRODUCTION

BY MIKHAIL GORBACHEV

Dear Reader—this global citizen's handbook for living on planet Earth speaks to you in person. Indeed, this is a message that is addressed to you and to all of us. It is written in the hope that you will not only read it, but will also think through the things it tells you. Furthermore that you will draw the necessary conclusions, your own conclusions, for yourself, your family, your friends, and everyone close to you.

Why did the author of this book, Ervin Laszlo—the famous scientist and humanist, and president of the Club of Budapest—choose this specific form, the form of a message addressed to us, to each and every one of us, his readers?

In general, when someone's future or some aspect of the world that surrounds us in daily life is in question, we see the gist of the issue fairly easily and quickly. We see the advantages and dangers and draw the conclusions, deciding what steps to take. This is natural, it corresponds with our habits, it is part of our everyday thinking and behavior. For someone living in a complex world, common sense dictates that he or she must think about whether or not to adapt to the given circumstances, or try to change them.

The situation is different when we confront problems that affect the whole of the world, the destiny of all humankind. We are not used to questions of such dimensions. It may seem that they are far away and that some time, somehow, they will be solved, indeed that someone up there is taking care of them. Why us? We are only little people.

This is why the book in your hand, dedicated to global, world-encompassing problems, addresses you in plain and logical language and marshals persuasive evidence. This makes our task easier. The task is simple. Get down to the basics, understand that global problems are not foreign to us. They are our problems. We are all touched by them, and touched by them not any less than we are by ordinary, everyday things. And it is we, each one of us, who not only can understand these problems, but can also do something significant to overcome them.

What Is At Stake?

The fact is that with the passing of time a whole pyramid of diverse problems has been accumulating in every part of the world: social, political, economic and cultural problems. Contradictions have appeared in society—in a different way in each country, but present all the same—and they have created conflicts and crises. Even wars. The relationship between man and nature has become more and more complex and strained. The air has become poisoned, rivers polluted, forests decimated. The number of contradictions keeps growing, and they are becoming deeper. Society is showing the symptoms of sickness.

In our various ways all of us, in every part of the world, have expressed our dissatisfaction with this state of affairs, have demanded changes, and are still demanding them. Isn't this story familiar? I think it is.

However, at a certain point these challenges and contradictions become so serious that changes become unavoidable. If the leaders who decide the life of society prove incapable of understanding the necessity for changes, and of doing something about it, people will not put up with them any longer. Violent movements will arise, such as strikes and disturbances. Society will enter a period of crisis. How will the crisis be resolved? This is difficult to predict. Society's sickness affects every single member, every single citizen, and threatens everyone with suffering. The end result may be an explosion, a bloodbath that nobody wants, yet which comes about spontaneously.

Another Way Out

Is there another way out, a path beyond the crisis? The book in your hand gives an answer: yes, there is another way. We must not wait until society's crisis reaches the danger point. We must act! Every person can act. If everyone does his or her bit, together we can accomplish what is necessary. We can make an impact on those who decide the politics and the destiny of society, and motivate them to begin making the necessary changes. Changes that not only resolve the crisis, but take us on a path of survival, of healthy development for people and nature, and a better quality of life for all. That is our salvation.

The human community has reached the point where it must decide whether it allows events to take their course (and if it does, we will all be put to a difficult test) or whether it manages to make the turning that changes the character and the content of development for the benefit of humankind. To make this decision, we must first become conscious that a turning is truly necessary. Then we must understand what we must do to avoid the worst, and how we must do it.

This book helps us to understand the current situation of our planet and to find the path we must take. It helps us determine what we must do and how we must do it to ensure our common well-being. The future that confronts us is an open future. All of us—and that includes you, the reader—can do our bit to decide it.

Read this handbook, and start thinking. This is essential for you, for your family, for your present or future children and grandchildren, for your friends, and for everyone around you.

꒜ PREFACE

Our world is divided and conflict-torn, socially and ecologically unsustainable. We cannot remain as we are, nor can we go back to conditions that are now behind us. We can only move forward, but not on the same path we have been following until now. We need to find a new direction for our individual and collective future in our individual and collective interest.

Finding a new path is a major challenge, but it can be met. Meeting it calls for answering two questions: first, *just what is at the root of all the conflict and crisis in today's world*; and second, *what can I and those around me actually do to move toward a world where we can live in peace, without marginalizing and killing each other and destroying the environment?* The Club of Budapest was founded in 1993 to bring together creative people with a "planetary ethics" and "planetary consciousness" to come up with answers to these questions.

Hence this book, a report by the Club of Budapest, gives you not only a concise and factual review of the problems that beset our times, but tells you what you can do about them. It is a handbook in the truest sense of the word: a book to be consulted when you ask yourself what it is that you can do to move towards peace and sustainability on this planet.

This is a realistic endeavor. Today's world not only needs changing, it is also unstable and hence changeable. And, as a surprising, and surprisingly positive, fall-out from the current crises of terrorism, war, poverty, and environmental degradation, the momentum for change is gathering. You can reinforce this momentum and help to guide it so it could take you, and all of us, on a path towards a better world.

This, then, is a book for young people and for people of all ages who are young in spirit and are willing to be change-catalysts of the urgently needed transformation towards peace and sustainability, locally as well as globally.

Budapest and Montescudaio,
May 2003

ERVIN LASZLO

ꙮ ONE

The World in Our Hands

The message of this book is simple. We must not wait for fundamental change to come from "above," from the elected or appointed leaders of contemporary society; meaningful change must come from "below," from the people who live in those societies. This is a realistic objective. Over the past few years, the prospects for such a grassroots movement have been greatly enhanced by two parallel developments: first, the need for fundamental change has become ever more urgent and apparent; and second, people all over the world have become increasingly willing to pursue such change.

Change will come, because humankind cannot go on as before. War and terrorism are only the tip of the iceberg. The submerged but now increasingly emerging body of the iceberg is the growing stress, frustration and hate generated by the impoverishment of our life-sustaining environment and the imbalance resulting from the workings of the world's economic and social system.

Change will come, for it must come, but when and how will it come? Predicting the timing and the form of the change awaiting us is not the challenge, for the future is not to be fore-told; it is to be created. The challenge facing us is to create a positive future. If we act wisely and effectively, we can create a more peaceful and sustainable world over the span of the next few years. We are not obliged to go on living in crisis and con-flict. The world need not remain violent, and economically, socially and ecologically unsustainable. We can progress towards harmony, cooperation, livable communities, and a value system that nourishes and sustains us and all things that live on this Earth.

If we want to better this world, we should be clear what is wrong with it. This is the first item on our agenda. We should look at the facts. Fortunately, the facts are known and they speak loud and clear.

The current globalized economic and social system has brought unparalleled wealth to a few and marginalization and misery to many. It has globalized production, trade, finance and communication, but it has also created national and regional unemployment, widening income gaps, and a mount-ing degradation of the local and the global environment. The benefits of economic growth, for long the main indicator of progress, have become ever more concentrated. While the richest 20% of the world's population become richer still, the poorest 20%, over 1.2 billion people, are pressed into absolute poverty, barely surviving on less than one dollar a day, in urban slums and shantytowns and in depressed rural hinterlands.

These conditions are explosive: they fuel resentment and revolt. As long as people harbor hate and the desire for revenge, they cannot co-exist peacefully and cooperatively. Whether the cause is the wounded ego of a person or the wounded self-respect of a people; whether it is the wish for personal revenge or a holy war in defense of a faith, the poten-tial for violence remains. Attaining peace in people's hearts is a precondition of attaining peace in the world. And inner peace depends very much on creating more equitable conditions on this planet.

4

Today's world is full of problems. In industrialized countries, job security is a thing of the past. In poor countries, poverty is aggravated by hunger, joblessness, and degrading conditions. Both rich and poor countries overwork productive lands, contaminate rivers, lakes and seas, and draw down water tables. And the gap between the modern and the traditional segments of society tears apart the structures and institutions on which social stability depends.

The contemporary world runs on money and is hooked on economic growth. Money might make the world go round, but it is not ordinary money that does the work: it is primarily "debt-money". Most of the money in the world—all but the three or four percent that we use in banknotes and coins in everyday commerce—is not issued by central banks and guaranteed by governments but is created by commercial banks in the form of credit. People ask for credit when they need more money and are confident that they can repay it; businesses borrow when they want to expand and believe that they can do so profitably. Economic growth fuels economic confidence and leads to an increase in borrowing—which means an increase in the amount of the debt-money that drives the system. The system is self-fuelling: debt, if it is to be repaid with interest, requires economic growth; growth leads to more lending and thus to more debt-money, which in turn leads to more growth—and more debt-money. In this system, rich people and multinational corporations are the main beneficiaries: they can qualify for credit and obtain debt-money. Poor people and small businesses are left on the margins.

Due to the self-perpetuating cycles of the world's monetary system, the rights endorsed by the world community—the right to health, nourishment, and employment spelled out in the International Covenant on Economic, Social and Cultural Rights—become more and more illusory. Although governments and various institutions pay lip-service to these rights, fewer and fewer people actually exercise them. Ensuring that all people have access to the conditions required for their health, nourishment and employment is not, and cannot be, a priority of modern governments. Governments need to work closely with banks and major businesses to maintain the momentum of growth in their economy: they are terrified by the prospect of stagnation and recession. National economies simply must grow if they are not to enter into a downward spiral. But in this system, maintaining the momentum of economic growth means more borrowing and more debt-money. This leaves poor people out of play and widens the gap between the wealthy and powerful, and the poor and powerless segments of society.

The money-driven global economy cannot keep growing indefinitely. Ultimately, this expanding bubble is bound to burst. But as long as it is expanding it increases the gap between the rich and the poor and feeds discontent and frustration in more than two-thirds of the world's population.

Lives and Fortunes in the Global Village

To appreciate the diversity of lives and fortunes in the global village, assume that it is made up of 1,000 inhabitants. 560 of them are women and 440 are men. Nearly 300 are younger than fifteen years of age, and 69 are older than sixty-five.

576 of the 1,000 inhabitants are Asians, 320 are Europeans, Americans, Arabs, and Australians, and 104 are Africans. 162 of them speak Chinese, 81 English, 69 Hindi, 65 Spanish, 52 Russian, 37 Arabic, and 34 Bengali—the rest speak one of the thousands of other tongues. 149 live on an average income of $78 a day, 445 live on $16/day, 406 try to live on $5/day, and 227 have to subsist somehow on $1/day. 140 are illiterate, 328 do not receive even a minimal health care, and 19 of the children have no access to a school. 25 are refugees, and 10 are leaving each year their native communities for the cities. The 200 better-off consume 86 percent of everything that

is on the market, while the poorest 800 consumes 14 percent. Each of the 149 "wealthy" uses 250 million liters of water in the course of his or her life, 15 million liters of gasoline, 45,000 kilos of steel, 65 tons of cereals, and the wood of 1,000 trees.

If current trends do not change, by the year 2050 there will be not 1,000, but 1,500 people in the global village. 690 of them will not have access to clean water and 300 will have less than $1 a day on which to survive.

Our world has become economically and socially unsustainable. But this is not all: as we know, the unsustainability of our world also has deep ecological roots. They reside in the serious and still growing imbalance between human habitations and the self-maintaining cycles of nature. In the past, this was not the case—or at least, the imbalance that came about was not critical, since the human exploitation of the environment was relatively modest. With primitive technologies and small populations the supply of natural resources seemed endless, and environmental damage insignificant. When an environment was unwittingly damaged, its resources over-exploited, there were other environments to conquer and to exploit.

In the middle of the 19th century the world's population reached one billion, and its impact on the environment increased dramatically. Both population and the use of natural resources grew continually throughout the 20th century. In the past 50 years, our parents and grandparents used more of nature's resources than in all of the preceding millennia put together. Today our global village has nearly six-and-a-half billion inhabitants. Yet the load we place on the environment is not due to our numbers, but to our irresponsible use of its resources. Our bodies constitute only 0.014% of the planet's biomass, and 0.44% of the biomass of animals. Our exploitation of the planet is entirely out of proportion to our numbers.

Consider the size of our "ecological footprint". This is the area of land required to support a human being, or a group of human beings. It defines the share of the planet's biological productivity used by an individual, a city, a nation, or all of humanity. If the footprint of a settlement is larger than its area, that settlement is not independently sustainable. A city is intrinsically unsustainable because very few of the natural resources used by its inhabitants come from within its boundaries. Most resources, such as food, water, minerals and fuels, come from beyond the city, from hinterlands, catchments, mines, and wells. But entire regions and countries could well be sustainable: their ecological footprint need not extend beyond their territories. This, however, is not the case.

In 1996, the Earth's biosphere had 12.6 billion hectares of biologically productive space, making up about one quarter of the planetary surface. It comprised 9.4 billion hectares of land and 3.2 billion hectares of fishing ground. Equitably shared, in a population of 5.7 billion this yielded an "Earth-share" of 2.18 hectares per person. Now we have grown to nearly six and a half

World Ecological Footprint

12.6 billion hectares of biologically productive space divided by population

Earth's Biological Capacity
1.9 hectares . . . .

African and Asian Consumer
1.4 hectares . . . .

World-wide Consumer
2.3 hectares . . . .

Western European Consumer
5.0 hectares . . . .

North American Consumer
9.6 hectares . . . .

Source: World Wildlife Fund's Living Planet Report 2000

billion, but the biosphere's biological productivity remained at best constant. Thus today's Earth-share would be 1.9 hectares for each man, woman and child on the planet. But the average ecological footprint comes to 2.8 hectares. Humanity exceeds its collective Earth-share by more than 30%.

The World Wildlife Fund's Living Planet Report 2000 examined the footprints of 151 nations, including the largest, most highly populated countries. There are 75 countries that consume above their Earth-share. They make up only 21% of humanity, but their over-consumption is large. The United Arab Emerites, Singapore, and the United States exceed their Earth-share five times—the average footprint in North America is 9.6 hectares. By contrast, the average footprint in Bangladesh is 0.5 hectares. If the footprint of the 42 rich countries were to be attained by all of the 189 formally constituted nation-states of the world, the global overshoot would be 100%. To remain in balance with our ecological base, we would require another planet the size of Earth!

We are approaching the outer edge of the Earth's capacity to sustain human life. The 2002 Living Planet report warned that we are plundering the planet at a pace that greatly outstrips its capacity to support life. More than a third of the natural resources of the world have been destroyed by human activity over the past three decades. If these trends were to continue, by the year 2050 we would need not one, but two other planets the size of Earth.

Humanity not only exploits, and indeed over-exploits nature, it also impairs it. The progressive degradation of the environment was not widely recognized until the 1980s. Prior to that, the success of technological civilization obscured the fact that the cycles of nature had become progressively degraded. Chemically-bolstered mechanized agriculture increased yields per acre and made more acres available for cultivation, but it also increased the growth of algae in lakes and waterways. Chemicals such as DDT proved to be effective insecticides, but they poisoned entire animal, bird, and insect

populations. We now produce 300 to 500 million tons of haz-
ardous waste and toxic chemicals each year, and when some
part of this reaches the environment it poisons people as well
as plants and animals. In industrialized countries we already
have between 500 and 1,000 times more than the normal level
of lead in our bodies. And we have polluted lakes and rivers and
drawn down water tables to the point where one in six in the
human family lacks clean drinking water and two in five do not
have adequate sanitation.

The Worldwatch Institute's 2003 State of the World
Report noted that because of encroachment by human habitation and, above all, pollution and over-exploitation, about
12% of the birds of the planet are presently in danger of
extinction, as are 25% of the mammals. The human species is
not immune to the dangers. The degradation of nature affects
human survival: one quarter of the developing world's agricultural land is seriously degraded and 420 million people now
live in countries that no longer have enough cropland to grow
their own food. About 30% of the world's remaining forests
are fragmented or degraded, and 50% of the world's wetlands
have been lost over the last one hundred years. As a result 500
million people live in regions of chronic drought. By the year
2025 that number is likely to increase more than fivefold, to
between 2.4 and 3.4 billion.

The ecological unsustainability of the world today is aggravated by the fact that ecosystems do not collapse piecemeal.
We have been operating on the assumption that in nature
cause and effect is proportional, so that an additional ounce of
pollution produces an additional ounce of damage. This, however, is not so. Ecosystems may be polluted for many years
without any change at all, then flip into an entirely different
condition. Gradual changes create cumulative vulnerability,
until a single shock to the system, such as a flood or a drought,
knocks the system into a different state, and that state may be
considerably less adapted to sustaining human life and economic activity.

A leap into a catastrophic new state can also occur in the global climate. According to a 2002 report by the U.S. National Academy of Sciences, abrupt changes come about when the climate system is forced to cross some critical threshold. We are now approaching such a threshold. There are a growing number of "hothouse gases" in the atmosphere, including 370.9 parts per million of carbon dioxide, which is the highest not only in recorded history, but very likely in the past 20 million years. Because of the sudden leaps that come about in ecosystem development, instead of occurring gradually over the course of the next 100 years, global warming (a rise in temperatures somewhere between 1.4 and 5.8 degrees centigrade) could happen in the next few years. The new climate could undermine human settlements and ecologies throughout the world. Forests may be consumed by fires, grasslands may dry out and turn into dust bowls, wildlife could disappear, and diseases such as cholera, malaria, dengue fever and yellow fever could decimate human populations.

The bottom line is that our global village is inequitable, full of frustration and hate, and is neither economically nor ecologically sustainable. This condition cannot be prolonged indefinitely. We either achieve peace and a higher level of sustainability, or risk a global holocaust.

Half a century ago Albert Einstein noted that we cannot solve a problem with the same kind of thinking that gave rise to it. Nobel scientists now agree. A Declaration signed by one hundred Laureates at the conclusion of the Nobel Peace Prize Centennial Symposium in December of 2001 noted, "The most profound danger to world peace in the coming years will stem not from the irrational acts of states or individuals but from the legitimate demands of the world's dispossessed."

They ended the Declaration saying, "To survive in the world we have transformed, we must learn to think in a new way".

New thinking is a "soft factor" in the life of society, but when it comes to deciding our future it carries more weight than money and power, the traditional "hard factors". The urgently required local and global transformation calls for timely changes in the way we think. With new, more responsible thinking we could head towards better, more peaceful and sustainable conditions on this planet. As Mikhail Gorbachev has made clear, when all is said and done, the world is in our hands.

♒ TWO

Breakdown or Breakthrough: A Choice of Futures

There is not just one possible future before us, but many. In the final count we face a negative future of breakdown, as well as a positive future of breakthrough. Which one will come about? This is not decided yet—the choice is still ours. Let us picture, then, these dramatically different scenarios step by step.

The Initial Conditions

The Critical Economic, Social, and Cultural Factors

- Increasing population pressure: 77 million humans added to the world population every year, 97% of them in poor countries
- Spreading poverty: nearly two billion people living on less than two dollars a day, more than one billion of them in urban slums at the lowest levels of physical subsistence
- Widening gap between rich and poor people as well as rich and poor economies: 80% of the human population

13

has but a 14% share of global consumption, while the richest 20% accounts for 86%

- Persistent religious/cultural intolerance in the Middle East, the Balkans, the Indian subcontinent, and other hot-spots
- Rising resentment of America's apparent hegemonic aspirations in the pursuit of global economic and political goals backed by military force
- Growing threat of terrorism and consequent armed retaliation

The Critical Ecological Factors

- Accelerating deforestation and reduction of biodiversity: disappearance of tropical rain forests, loss of an untold number of species, monocultures on cultivated lands
- Accelerating climate change, with extremes of cold and heat, violent storms and changed rainfall patterns
- Worsening industrial, urban, and agricultural pollution: changed chemical composition of the atmosphere, desalination and impoverishment of agricultural lands, and lowering and poisoning of water tables
- Rising sea levels: loss of low-lying plains and river valleys in Southern Asia, flooding of island countries in the Pacific, and threat to coastal cities throughout the world

The Breakdown Scenario

2005–2010: The First Steps Toward Breakdown

- Fundamentalism fed by resentment over perceived economic and social injustice generates holy wars in the Muslim world
- Terrorism spreads, together with attempts to eliminate terrorists by attacking the countries that harbor them

- The North Atlantic alliance linking Europe, the United States and Russia collapses
- France, Germany, Russia, and China form a coalition to balance what they perceive as growing U.S. military-economic hegemony, joined by Brazil, India, South Korea, and other developing countries
- Sharp rise in global military spending, as on the one hand the U.S. and its allies, and on the other the alternative bloc countries, enter the spiral of arms competition
- Global economic stagnation combined with U.S. unilateralism weakens the International Monetary Fund and the World Trade Organization, and as regional economic agreements become more attractive than multilateral trade arrangements and bilateral trade with the U.S., trade wars become frequent and increasingly destabilizing

2010–2015: Deepening Chaos

- Water and food shortages in Sub-Saharan Africa, China, Southern Asia, and Meso-America generate water- and hunger-wars
- Starvation and unsanitary conditions accelerate the spread of HIV/AIDS, SARS, and other epidemics
- Millions of climate refugees from flooded coastal cities, low-lying areas, and destitute urban and rural regions move towards North America and Europe
- North-South trade agreements are cancelled and trade flows disrupted; the international economic/financial system is in shambles
- Corruption as well as maverick and organized crime spread on the six continents

2015–2020: The Advent of Global Holocaust

- Political and economic conflict between the U.S. and its allies and the alternative military-economic bloc reaches

Two Scenarios

BREAKDOWN

BREAKTHROUGH

Global Armed
Conflict Involving
Weapons of
Mass Destruction

More Equitable
Distribution
of Resources

2020

Development of
Renewable
Energy Programs

Environmental
Devastation

Widespread Reform of
Governmental and
Corporate Structures

2010

Epidemics

Cooperation and
Dialogue Replacing
International
Conflict

Widespread Shortages

2000

1990

Climate Change

Pollution

Religious Intolerance

Environmental Crisis

War

Terrorism

Gap Between
Rich and Poor

Threats of
Social Breakdown

Population Growth

Poverty

1950s

a crisis point; hawks and armaments lobbies on both sides press for the use of weapons of mass destruction
- Strong-arm régimes come to power in the developing world, determined to use armed force to right perceived wrongs
- Regional wars erupt in the traditional hot-spots and spread to neighboring countries
- The major military-political-economic power-blocs use hi-tech weaponry to achieve conflicting economic and political objectives
- Some of the newly arising strong-arm régimes insert nuclear, chemical, or biological weapons to resolve regional conflicts
- War fought with conventional and non-conventional weapons escalates to the global level; the international economic and financial system is in chaos; political relations among states break down; anarchy and destruction become generalized

The Breakthrough Scenario

2005–2010: The First Steps Toward a Breakthrough

- The experience of terrorism and war, together with rising poverty and a variety of environmental threats and disasters, triggers positive changes in the way people think; the idea that people themselves can be effective agents of transformation toward a more peaceful and sustainable world captures the imagination of individuals in more and more societies; people in different cultures and different walks of life pull together to confront the threats they face in common
- The worldwide rise of popular movements for peace and international cooperation leads to the election of similarly motivated political figures, lending fresh impetus to projects of economic cooperation and intercultural understanding

17

- An electronic E-Parliament comes on line, linking parliamentarians worldwide and providing a forum for debates on the best ways to serve the common good
- Non-governmental organizations link up through the Internet and develop shared strategies to restore peace and revitalize war-torn regions and environments; they promote socially and ecologically responsible policies in local and national governments and in business
- Local, national and global businesses respond to the increasingly forceful calls by government and civic society for corporate social and ecological responsibility

2010–2015: The Crystallizing Contours of Peace and Cooperation

- Money is re-assigned from military and defense budgets to fund practical attempts at conflict resolution
- Reforms are undertaken in the world's monetary system: a world currency is put into circulation by the reformed World Bank Group on the basis of population size rather than financial power, creating a more equitable flow of money among the world's disparate economies
- Agriculture is restored to a place of primary importance in the economy, both for producing staple foods and for growing energy crops and raw materials for communities and industry
- A worldwide renewable energy program is created, paving the way toward a third industrial revolution making use of solar and other renewable energy sources to transform the global economy and lift marginalized populations out of the vicious cycles of poverty

2015–2020: The Emerging Foundations of a New World

- National, continental and global governance structures are reformed or freshly created, moving states toward

18

participatory democracy and releasing a surge of creative energy among empowered and increasingly active populations

- The consensually created, locally autonomous but globally coordinated and cooperative economic-political system begins to function
- As a consequence, international and intercultural mistrust, ethnic conflict, racial oppression, economic injustice, and gender inequality give way to a higher level of trust, and a shared will by the world's peoples to achieve peaceful relations among states and a significant level of sustainability in the economy and the environment*

These scenarios illustrate the futures that can come about in today's unstable and unsustainable world. It is not the initial conditions that decide among them—the world from which they take off is the same; it is today's world. The difference is in the way people respond to conditions in this world. As Einstein knew, the decisive factor is not the problem, but the way we think about it.

In today's near-chaotic world, new thinking can make a crucial difference. The shape of tomorrow will be decided by how we think today. Just as the legendary flap of the wings of a butterfly can create an air current that amplifies and amplifies until it changes the weather on the other side of the globe, in a condition of chaos and instability local and seemingly marginal actions can produce decisive "butterfly effects". Such actions can, and very likely will, decide whether humankind embarks on a scenario of breakthrough, or remains mired on a path leading to breakdown.

Two Ways of Thinking and Acting

In the course of history people have thought in widely different

---

* The kind of world the scenario of breakthrough could produce by the year 2020 and beyond is depicted in chapter 5.

ways about themselves and the world around them. There were different conceptions of society, life, honor, and dignity in the East and in the West, in classical epochs, in the Middle Ages, and in the Modern Age. This kind of diversity has not disappeared with the advent of industrial civilization. Surveys of public opinion and preferred lifestyles in the United States show that, despite the international image created by the policies of the Bush administration, a surprisingly large number of Americans think and live in a peace-loving and sustainability-oriented way. A new culture is emerging in America: the "cultural creatives".[1] The contrast between this culture and the mainstream "moderns" is real and merits a more detailed look.

Who Are the Moderns?

In 1999 the "moderns" made up 48% of the American people: some 93 million out of about 193 million adults, more men than women. Family income was in the region of $40,000 to $50,000 per year, situating them in the upper-middle income bracket. Moderns share many of the traditional virtues and values of Americans. They believe in God, in being honest, in the importance of family and education, and in a fair day's pay for a fair day's work. Moderns aspire to—

- climb the ladder of success with measurable steps
- make or have a lot of money
- look good and be on top of the latest trends
- be entertained by the media

They are convinced that—

- the body is much like a machine
- organizations, too, are much like machines
- either big business or big government is in control, and knows best
- bigger is better
- what can be measured is what gets done
- analyzing things into their parts is the best way to solve a problem

- efficiency and speed are the top priorities—time is money
- life can be compartmentalized into separate spheres: work, family, socializing, making love, education, politics, and religion
- being concerned with spirituality and the inner dimensions of life is flaky and immaterial to the real business of living

And These Cultural Creatives?

The cultural creatives have a different set of values, beliefs and aspirations, and adopt correspondingly different lifestyles. In 1999, this emerging culture had a 23.4% share of the U.S. adult population, including almost twice as many women as men, with the majority coming from the middle or the affluent classes.

- Cultural creatives buy more books and magazines than moderns, listen to more radio, preferably news and classical music, and watch less television
- They are aggressive consumers of the arts and culture, more likely to go out and get involved, whether as amateurs or professionals
- Creatives want the whole story of whatever they get in their hands, from cereal boxes to magazine articles; they dislike superficial advertising and product description, wanting to know how things originated, how they were made, who made them, and what will happen to them when they are discarded
- Cultural creatives want real goods and services; they have led the consumer rebellion against products considered fake, imitation, throwaway, cliché, or merely fashionable
- The creatives do not buy on impulse but research what they consume, reading labels and assuring themselves that they are getting what they want; they do not simply buy the latest gadgets and innovations on the market

- Cultural creatives are consumers of intense, enlightening, or enlivening experience such as weekend workshops, spiritual gatherings, personal growth events, and experiential vacations
- Cultural creatives want their homes to be as ecologically balanced as possible, avoiding status displays and wanting to create a nest with interesting nooks and niches; they like to work at home
- The common thread among the creatives is their "holism", shown in their preference for natural whole foods, holistic health care, whole-system information, and a holistic balance between work, play, consumption and inner growth
- With regard to material products, cultural creatives prefer ecologically sound and efficient goods, such as fuel-efficient, relatively non-polluting cars that can also be recycled

The creatives consider themselves synthesizers and healers, not just on the personal level but also in the community, at a national and even a global level. They aspire to create change in personal values and public behavior that could shift the dominant culture beyond the fragmented and mechanistic world of the moderns.

Similar new cultures are growing in other parts of the world. A survey by the European Union's monthly Euro-Barometer questioned people in 15 of the Union's member states regarding their cultural and lifestyle preferences, and found that creatives are present in Europe in much the same proportion as in the U.S. [2]

These are hopeful developments. People who belong to the new cultures abhor war and violence in all its forms. They place less pressure on the environment and are more open to understanding others and cooperating with them. Their lifestyles are simpler, not for lack of money, but because of an intrinsic preference for simplicity and authenticity. All this means that more creatives than moderns could live on the planet without triggering terrorism, engaging in warfare, creating religious and cultural conflicts, and provoking resource shortages and environmental degradation.

NOTES

1. See Paul H. Ray and Sherry Ruth Anderson, *The Cultural Creatives* (Harmony Books, New York, 2000). The third culture identified in their survey was that of the "traditionals". Members of this culture had family incomes in the relatively low range of $20,000 to $30,000 per year, due among other things to the reduced income of the many retirees among them. Traditionals are less relevant to the choice of futures before us than the other cultures. The mainly backward-looking ideals of older people are not being taken up by the younger generation, and this population is dwindling.

2. More definitive figures will be established by the European Survey of Planetary Consciousness of the Club of Budapest in Germany, Italy, France, Norway, Poland, and Hungary. Further surveys are projected for Japan and Brazil.

↬ THREE

Think Responsibly

New, more adapted ways of thinking are spreading in the world, but it is by no means certain that they will spread fast enough. If you, a responsible global citizen, are to play your part in catalyzing and promoting a grass-roots movement toward a peaceful and sustainable world, you must be sure to think in a new and better way.

Start with yourself. The first step is to reexamine your ethics. Ask yourself: Is the way I think about right and wrong *really* sound and up-to-date? Are the things I judge worthy and good *truly* good and worth striving for?

A Question of Ethics

What we hold to be right and good cannot be dictated by anyone, be it parent, priest, teacher, boss, or political leader. We must decide our ethics for ourselves. In a democratic society a wide variety of opinions can be held and a great many goals pursued. But there is a limit to our freedom to define our ethics: what we hold to be right and good must mesh with what is right and good for the communities in which we live. Today we live not only in a local community—a village, town, or city. We live not only in one state and nation, and not even in just one region and culture. We live in an interacting and interdependent global village. Our ethics must also mesh with what is right and good for humanity.

Yet, with the notable exception of the new cultures, the global dimension is missing in people's ethics. This is evident in the way they live, or aspire to live. As we have seen, when multiplied by the number of people in the world, the ecological footprint of individuals is larger than the total biological productivity of the planet. Modern lifestyles have become globally unsustainable, and pursuing an unsustainable way of living cannot be considered ethical.

Without a global dimension to people's ethics humankind faces difficult times. A statement signed by 1,670 scientists from 70 countries made this point. "A great change in our stewardship of the Earth and the life on it is required if vast human misery is to be avoided and our global home on this planet is not to be irretrievably mutilated."[1] The scientists, including 102 Nobel laureates, concluded that a global ethics must motivate a great movement to convince reluctant leaders and governments, and reluctant peoples themselves, to effect the needed changes.

A global or planetary ethics is not partisan, serving one country or culture above others. The basic principle is to treat others—*all* others—as you expect others to treat you. This is a universal "golden rule" expressed in all the great religions of humankind. In Christianity it was pronounced by Jesus: "In everything, do to others as you would have them do to you." In Judaism the golden rule is expressed in the Talmud: "What is hateful to you, do not do to your neighbor," and in Islam it is present in Mohammed's tenet, "Not one of you truly believes until you wish for others that which you wish for yourself." Hinduism says, "This is the sum of duty: do not do to others what would cause pain if done to you"; the Buddha advised,

"Treat not others in ways that you yourself would find hurtful;" and Confucius said "Do not do to others what you do not want done to yourself."[2]

In the tradition, "you" has stood for neighbor, friend, and fellow member of the local community. That was the range within which people interacted. Today the range of human interaction is global: what any of us does affects all the others. Our ethics must expand as well. What any member of the global community does must not be injurious to any other member of this community.

We are far from attaining this goal. What some people do is in fact injurious to the rest of the global community, even if they do not do it on purpose. The rich use up an inordinate share of the planet's resources and produce the lion's share of its waste and pollution, and the poor are forced to over-exploit the lands, waters and forests that surround their habitation. If these practices continue we shall soon be missing essential resources and live in an impoverished and dramatically unhealthy environment.

The lesson is clear: if you do not want others to violate your right to a healthy environment and to a fair share of the planet's resources, you must not degrade other people's environment and interfere with their access to basic resources. In today's world, "Do as you would be done by " becomes "Live in a way that allows all people on the planet to live" (and not just subsist at the edge of starvation).

Adopting this planetary ethics does not mean that you must live in poverty, or even with extreme frugality. All people do not need to live at the same material standard you do; they may not even want to. The goal is not uniformity, but fairness. We can aim for fairness in the world without depriving ourselves of the pleasures and enjoyment of a reasonable and responsible life. We can strive for personal excellence, growth, and enjoyment, even for comfort and non-wasteful luxury. We must simply define the pleasures and achievements of life in relation to the quality of responsible enjoyment and genuine satisfaction

27

they provide, rather than in terms of the amount of money they cost and the quantity of materials and energy they require. Then we give a fair chance to all people in the world to live with a decent measure of dignity and well-being.

The Matter of Beliefs

A more timely planetary ethics may still seem like an arbitrary imposition if it is not rooted in the way you look at the world and at your place and role in the world. This calls for also examining your beliefs. We all hold beliefs, whether they are sound or illusory, and whether we are aware of them or not. The challenge is to hold beliefs that are warranted by the reality we are now living.

20th Century Beliefs

Are the beliefs you hold up-to-date—or are they outdated? In the first decade of the 21st century many of the cherished beliefs of the 20th century became obsolete. Could it be that some of the beliefs you hold are among them? Here is a simple checklist:

- We are all separate individuals enclosed by our skin; if I cooperate it is only to promote my own interests
- There is only one country and one people to whom I owe allegiance; its interests take precedence over the interests of other countries
- The duty of my government is to ensure my country's economic and political interests with all the power it has at its disposal
- Freedom and justice in the world are best assured by the workings of the free market, and this should be brought about by economic incentives or, if necessary, by the use of force
- Women's place is in the home; in the workplace women are best at assisting men, keeping order, or cleaning up
- The value of everything, including human beings, can be calculated in money

---

Corresponding 20th and 21st Century Beliefs

20th Century Beliefs	21st Century Beliefs
1. We are all separate individuals	1. The struggle of each individual against all others is a threat to both winners and losers
2. I only owe allegiance to one country and one people	2. All of us belong to the global community
3. The free market is supreme and should be imposed by force if necessary	3. The combination of market fundamentalism with the force of arms is dangerous
4. A woman's place is in the home	4. The equal contribution of women is critical to the success of society
5. The value of everything, including humans, can be calculated monetarily	5. Adopting non-material values and simpler lifestyles is more responsible and makes better sense
6. Newer is always better	6. Novelty for its own sake leads to wasteful and unnecessary goods
7. The future is none of my business	7. Living without concern for the future is irresponsible
8. Crisis in the world is temporary and reversible	8. The world is undergoing rapid and fundamental transformation

---

- What every economy needs is growth, and what every person wants is to get rich
- Newer is always better; it is desirable, and for the economy even necessary, to buy and use the latest products and technologies; they make our economy grow and then everybody is better off
- The future is none of my business; every generation, like every person, has to look after itself
- Crisis in the world is reversible; the problems we are experiencing are temporary interludes, after which everything will get back to normal; business as unusual has evolved out of business as usual, and will sooner or later reverse back into it

29

21st Century Beliefs

A moment's reflection will tell you that such beliefs are obsolete.

- Seeing ourselves as individuals, separate and distinct from the social and the natural world in which we live, converts our natural impulse to seek our advantage into a short-sighted struggle among ever more unequal competitors. In today's inequitable yet interdependent world, engaging in this kind of struggle is not just unfair, it is a threat to both winners and losers.

- Believing that we owe allegiance to one country and one people only is a narrow form of patriotism. In reality we belong to many spheres and communities at the same time: we belong to a village or town, a culture or ethnic group, perhaps a business or industry, as well as to a nation. Some of these groups and communities are part of our country, others extend beyond it. In some parts of the world there are regional groupings, such as the European Union, and they also claim people's allegiance. And all of us belong to the global community of all peoples and countries. Acting on the premise of an exclusive national allegiance only provokes resentment and invites resistance on the part of other countries and cultures.

- The attempt to enforce the workings of the free market through economic incentives has a fair chance to work, but attempting to use military means to enforce our conceptions on other countries seldom if ever leads to freedom and justice—it only leads to resentment, opposition, conflict, and terrorism. In today's world combining the ideology of market fundamentalism with the doctrine of global military supremacy is a prelude to political crisis and economic chaos.

- Relegating women to secondary tasks at work is part of a dangerously unbalanced perception. It ignores women's enormous and essential capacity for seeing things in context, and for championing so-called soft factors such as values, ethics, caring, and sustainability.

30

These are crucial components of success in our unstable and crisis-prone world.

- The reduction of everything and everybody to economic value may have made sense when the rapid growth of the economy pushed everything else into the background. But it is obsolete in today's world, where more and more people are adopting non-material values, simpler lifestyles, and voluntarily modest forms of consumption.

- Worshipping novelty is based on the mistaken belief that whatever is newer, consumes more energy and materials, and is more expensive, must be better. This belief leads to a plethora of unnecessary services and wasteful goods, some of which only make life more complicated, stressful, or unhealthy.

- Living without conscious concern about the future made sense in periods of stability and growth, when it seemed that every generation could ensure a good life for itself, but it is irresponsible in a world in which our lifestyle and consumption choices and professional and civic behaviors have a major, and perhaps irreversible, impact on the world we bequeath to our children.

- Lastly, the belief that nothing changes fundamentally constrains creativity and makes us unable to learn from living in a world that is in rapid transformation, whether we know it or not

Five Nearly Lethal Beliefs

1. The Neolithic Illusion: Nature Is Inexhaustible

The belief that nature is a limitless resource goes back thousands of years. Originally, this faith in the inexhaustibility of nature was understandable and innocuous. Human tribes and groups did not overstep the limits of nature's capacity to regenerate the required resources; they lived in balance with their environment. This changed with the advent of the

31

Neolithic Era, about 10,000 years ago. In the Fertile Crescent, now the Middle East, people were not content to live within the rhythms and cycles of nature but sought ways to harness the forces of their environment. In some places, such as ancient Sumer, their practices had vexing consequences. In deforested lands, flash floods washed away irrigation channels and dams and left fields arid. Over the course of millennia of cultivation, the Fertile Crescent of biblical times became an arid region dominated by sandy desert. But it did not occur to the people of ancient Babylon, Sumer, Egypt, India and China that their environment could ever cease to supply them with edible plants, domestic animals, clean water and breathable air, or be fouled by waste and garbage. Nature seemed far too vast to be tainted, polluted, or defiled by human activity. This insight did not dawn on people until Rachel Carson published her pathbreaking *Silent Spring* in the 1970s.

Persisting in the Neolithic Illusion is dangerous and potentially even lethal. It leads us to squander nature's resources and overload its self-regenerative cycles. In early times this was not an insuperable problem, for people could move on, colonizing new lands and exploiting fresh resources. But in the 21st century when we over-exploit and destroy one environment after another, we have nowhere left to go.

2. Social Darwinism: the Ideology of Competitive Fitness

Another age-old belief, the idea that competition is the basis of all life, was given fresh impetus by Darwin's theory of evolution through natural selection. The social application of Darwin's theory, "Social Darwinism", holds that in society, as in nature, a competitive selection process eliminates the unfit: only the fit survive. This is taken to mean that if we want to survive we have to be fit for the existential struggle—fitter than our competitors. In society fitness is not determined by genes. It is a personal and cultural trait, expressed as smartness, daring, ambition, and the ability to garner money and put it to work.

In the 1930s and early '40s Social Darwinism was an inspiration of the Nazi ideology. It justified the conquest of foreign territories in the name of creating *Lebensraum* (living space) for Germany, and was put forward as a justification of the genocide of Jews, Slavs and Gypsies: the fitness—defined as the racial purity—of the Aryan race was to be preserved. In our day Social Darwinism has not disappeared, although it is not as virulent as in Nazi Germany. Armed might is still used to secure perceived interests, whether they are territorial, cultural, or economic.

In today's world the struggle for survival also takes another form: it emerges in the subtler but equally merciless struggle of competitors in the world of business. In this struggle, fitness rewards corporate executives, international financiers, and speculators: they become rich and powerful. The resulting gap between rich and poor creates frustration and issues in violence, but for the present the "fit" can pretend not to notice these consequences. The economic variant of Social Darwinism is nearly as noxious as its military variant.

3. Market Fundamentalism: Whatever the Question, the Market is the Answer

In the industrialized world mainstream business and political leaders elevate the market to the status of a tribal god. They accept pollution and global warming as the unavoidable cost of free-market competition; they sacrifice to it farmlands, forests, wetlands and prairies, ecosystems and watersheds. They justify their stance by maintaining that the market distributes benefits, so if one corporation or one country's economy thrives, other companies and countries will do well, too.

The "ideology of the market"—which, in practice becomes unwittingly the *idolatry* of the market—rests on a handful of fundamental beliefs.

- All human needs and wants can be expressed in monetary terms and can enter the market as a form of demand with a corresponding supply. Satisfying demand fuels the economy and is good for everybody.

- The human needs and wants that make up demand are fundamentally unlimited: there are no insuperable human, financial, or natural limits to the conversion of needs and wants into saleable commodities.
- Competition on the open market is both necessary and good: it is the governing principle of all economic and social relations.
- The freedom to compete on the market is the basis of human liberty and the foundation of social and economic justice

These are the tenets of market fundamentalism, and they are wrong. They leave out of account *first*, that we live on a finite planet with finite human and natural resources and a finite capacity to absorb the waste and pollution that accompanies most forms of industrial production, and *second*, that competition in the open market favors the rich at the expense of the poor. Everybody knows the adverse effects of waste and pollution; we see them on the climate, on the quality of air, water, and land, and on the regenerative capacity of crops, pastures, fishing grounds, and forests. Economists, in turn, know that the market distributes benefits only under conditions of near-perfect competition where the playing field is level and all players have more or less the same number of chips. It is evident that in today's world the field is far from level and the chips are far from evenly distributed. Even entering the market calls for money, and with few exceptions, money in the form of credit is accessible only to those who already have money, or can offer substantial collateral.

Market fundamentalism is a dangerous and ultimately lethal belief. Our precious but small planet sets limits to the purely quantitative, indiscriminate forms of economic growth, and the open market economy races toward these limits, making the rich still richer and swelling the numbers of the poor. It is hardly surprising that we are having growing resource shortages and environmental problems, and that the richest 20% of humankind earn 90 times more than the poorest 20%.

4. Consumerism: The More You Have, the Better You Are

This typically modern belief justifies the struggle for profit and wealth. It tells us that there is an equivalence between the size of our wallet, as demonstrated by our ability to acquire material possessions, and our personal worth as the owner of the wallet and the goods it can buy.

In the past, the equation of human worth with wealth and the consumption of material goods was consciously fueled by business. Companies held up conspicuous consumption as the ideal. Writing in 1950s America, Victor Lebov, a retailing analyst declared, "Our enormously productive economy demands that we make consumption our way of life, that we convert the buying and use of goods into rituals, that we seek our spiritual satisfaction, our ego satisfaction, in consumption. The economy needs things consumed, burned, worn out, replaced, and discarded at an ever-increasing rate."[3]

Today we know that consumerism is a false ideology. It leads to over-consumption and resource-depletion, and is neither healthy nor sustainable. The hoarding of material possessions by an individual, the same as the single-minded pursuit of natural and financial resources by a country, is a sign of insecurity and not of wisdom and integrity.

5. Militarism: The Way to Peace is Through War

The ancient Romans had a saying: if you aspire to peace, prepare for war. This matched their conditions and experience. The Romans had a worldwide empire, with rebellious peoples and cultures within and barbarian tribes at the periphery. Maintaining this empire required a constant exercise of military power. Today the nature of power is very different, but the belief about war is much the same. Like Rome in classical times, the United States is a global power, but one which is

35

economic rather than political. Maintaining it requires not armed enforcement but fair and sustainable relations between the world's remaining superpower and the rest of the international community.

This insight needs to dawn on the U.S. President along with other world leaders. Wise people have pointed to it already. Gandhi said that acting on the principle of an eye for an eye and a tooth for a tooth ends up making everyone blind and toothless. The Dalai Lama has remarked that today the world is so small and interdependent that war has become anachronistic, an outmoded approach—it should be relegated to the dustbin of history. The Pope has likewise condemned war as an instrument of national policy. The statement endorsed by the Members of the Club of Budapest (reproduced in the Appendix) goes still further: it affirms that in today's world, war is a crime against humanity.

We can see the futility of war and violence when we think of relations among individuals instead of states. Take a boardroom or council chamber. The agenda of the people around the table calls for dialogue and negotiation—the problems they face require shared decision and cooperative action. But some in the group hide a gun in their pocket, thinking they can prevail by threatening the others. Others in the group suspect this and pull their own guns to disarm those who might become aggressive. Still others feel that such preventive action is an aggression in itself; before using one's guns, those who hide arms should be given a chance to surrender them. But those with the biggest guns decide to use them. Then the whole table becomes polarized—some side with the big guns, others go against them. Bedlam erupts; shared decisions and cooperative actions are out of the question. Since everyone around the table owns guns, the situation can soon get out of hand.

When it comes to relations among states, the dynamics are similar, but the outcome is more dramatic. The lives of entire populations are at stake. The consequences of violent or violence-provoking actions are suffered not by those who make the decisions, but by the millions and billions whose interests they are supposed to represent.

In any event, in an economically divided and hate-filled world, investing in armaments and war is a poor choice. Global military expenditures already top $800 billion a year; the United States alone spends more than $340 billion, not counting the additional $135 billion for the war on Iraq. Yet war has nowhere led to peace and stability, not in the Balkans and in Central America, not in Africa and in the Middle and Far East.

The Five Nearly-Lethal Beliefs

1. **The Neolithic Illusion**
   The illusion that nature is infinite and inexhaustible; it could render the planet incapable of providing for the essential needs of humanity

2. **Social Darwinism**
   The naïve concept that unbridled competition is the law of life, in society as in nature; it provides a justification for the neglect of those most in need of help

3. **Market Fundamentalism**
   The belief that the market is the answer to every question leads to the over-exploitation of the planet's resources and exacerbates the gap between rich and poor

4. **Consumerism**
   The confusion of human worth with the consumption and ownership of material goods. It is neither healthy nor sustainable

5. **Militarism**
   An outdated concept, because in today's world, acting on the principle of an eye for an eye and a tooth for a tooth does not ensure peace and stability; it only makes people blind and toothless

---

War, however, is not the only way to peace and stability. According to estimates by the United Nations, starvation and the worst forms of malnutrition could be eliminated from the face of the Earth with an annual investment of about $19 billion; shelter could be provided for the world's homeless for $21 billion; clean water could be provided for everyone for about $10 billion; deforestation could be halted for $7 billion; global warming could be prevented for $8 billion and soil erosion for $24 billion. Investing in such programs for a period of ten years would go a long way towards alleviating frustration and mitigating resentment in the world, and would prove to be far more effective in paving the way to stability and peace than funding military campaigns to kill terrorists and attack unfriendly states and uncooperative régimes.

Singly and in combination, the beliefs that dominate the mind of the dominant layer of modern society are obsolete and dangerous. They tell us that our responsibilities end with satisfying our needs and the demands of our economy; that other people are none of our business and we can do as we please with nature; and they blind us to our obligations towards the wider human community and the life-supporting environment.

The Neolithic Illusion, Social Darwinism, Market Fundamentalism, Consumerism, and Militarism are especially dangerous, as they are powerful beliefs that appear in combination. For example, Market Fundamentalism and Militarism motivate much of the Bush administration's foreign policy, and the Neolithic Illusion and Consumerism continue to inspire the public relations of the majority of consumer goods manufacturers and retailers. The economic variant of Social Darwinism, in turn, goes hand in hand with Market Fundamentalism and Consumerism in the competitive environment of both business and politics. Small wonder that nature is suffering, and that our own world is inequitable and prone to violence!

NOTES
1. Statement of the Union of Concerned Scientists, 1993.
2. Sources for the Golden Rule citations:
      Christianity: Matthew 7:12;
      Judaism: Talmud, Shabbat 31a;
      Islam: The Prophet Muhammad, Hadith;
      Hinduism: Mahabharata 5:1517
      Buddhism: The Buddha, Udana-Varga 5.18;
      Zoroastrianism: Shayast-Na-Shayast 13.29;
      Confucianism: Confucius, Analects 15.23.
3. Quoted by Alan Durning in *How Much is Enough?* (Norton, 1992).

ॐ FOUR

Act Responsibly

Adopting a planetary ethics and updating our beliefs about the world are new and timely ways in which we must think. When we begin to think in this way, we will soon ask ourselves: *how can I live up to my new ethics and view of the world? In what way can I act more responsibly?*

Things We Can and Should Do

Seeking an answer to these questions is urgent, for some of the things we can, and as responsible people should do, brook no delay. If we wish to live and act responsibly, we must choose a path that leads toward sustainability and peace on this planet. This does not call for undue sacrifice, for there is no contradiction between doing good and doing well. If you live and act in a way that is good for others and for nature, you live and act in a way that is good for you.

Nobody is an island. How we live and what we do affects others around us. There are urgent and responsible things we can do in our private life, in our relations to the sphere of

41

business, as well as in the civic sphere of society. These are things we should do, for in an interdependent and interacting world each of us is a factor in the life of all.

Things We Can and Should Do in the Private Sphere

Some aspects of our private lives have become public business. These aspects are subject to the "ten commandments" of responsible living:

1. Live in a way that satisfies your needs without detracting from the opportunity of other people to satisfy theirs.

2. Live in a way that respects the right to life and development of all people, wherever they live, and whatever their ethnic origin, sex, citizenship, and belief system.

3. Live in a way that safeguards the right to life and a healthy environment of all the things that live and grow on this Earth.

4. Pursue happiness, freedom, and personal fulfillment in consideration of the similar pursuits of your fellows in your community, country and culture, and in the global community of all peoples, countries, and cultures.

5. Do your best to help those less privileged than you to live without hunger and penury, whether they live next door to you or in another part of the world.

6. Join with like-minded people to preserve or restore the integrity of the environment so it can generate and regenerate the resources essential for human life and well-being.

7. Help children and young people to discover sustainable ways of thinking and acting of their own.

8. Ask of your government that it deal peacefully and cooperatively with other nations and cultures, recognizing the legitimate aspirations for a better life and a life-supporting environment of all the peoples, countries, and cultures of the world.

"THE TEN COMMANDMENTS OF RESPONSIBLE LIVING"

I
Satisfy your needs without detracting from others

2
Live to respect the right to life and development of others

3
Safeguard the right to life and health of all growing and living things

4
Pursue happiness, freedom and fulfillment for self and in others

5
Help those less privileged to live without hunger and penury

6
Preserve or restore the integrity of the environment

7
Help children and young to discover ways of thinking and acting of their own

8
Ask your government to deal peacefully and cooperatively with other nations and cultures

9
Patronize businesses that provide without impairing the environment

IO
Use media with reliable information on trends and events that affect life to make sound decisions

9. Patronize businesses that produce goods and offer services that satisfy your needs and the needs of other people without impairing the environment and widening the gap between rich and poor in your community, and in the world at large.

10. Give preference to newspapers and magazines, television and radio programs and Internet sites that provide regular and reliable information on the trends and events that affect your life, and help you and others around you make informed decisions on crucial issues affecting your future.

We also need to improve our style of life. Here are five basic "commandments" of a responsible lifestyle:

i. When choosing products for yourself, instead of throwaway items that use a great deal of energy and raw material, give preference to functional devices that are made to last, are locally produced, and do the job with minimum waste of energy and materials.

ii. When choosing your work or profession, rather than striving to amass the most money in the shortest time, commit your time and talents to an activity that is useful and beneficial to community and country, and does not harm humans and nature.

iii. When selecting the furnishings of your home, instead of looking for items that show the neighbors how much you can afford, choose natural materials that last and make for warmth and sociability in your home.

iv. When choosing clothes, avoid unhealthy synthetic materials, and rather than looking for conspicuous and ostentatious labels, strive to express your personality, and the values of your culture and community.

v. When deciding on your daily diet, rather than choosing unhealthy and carelessly produced junk foods, choose organically and, where possible, locally grown products that provide healthy nourishment and do not despoil the environment. Remember: one hundred million people could be sustained by the land, water, and energy saved if Americans ate just 10% less meat. (It takes 25 gallons of water to produce one pound of wheat, but 5,214 gallons of water plus 16 pounds of grain and soy to produce one pound of beef!)

These things are not difficult to do, and they do not call for major sacrifices. On the contrary, they bring many benefits. We become a better neighbor and friend, and we live more healthily—by eating less meat, for example, we drastically reduce our chances of a heart attack. And we have the satisfaction of knowing that we are doing our best to be a responsible member of our community, our country, and the whole human family.

Things We Can and Should Do in the Sphere of Business

Interacting with Industrial Companies

The things we can and should do in the sphere of business are just as important as those in our private life, and they can be just as effective. Acting responsibly in regard to a business does not require being a business person—it is enough that we are a consumer, a client, a member of the community where businesses operate, and perhaps a shareholder in a company.

Interacting with companies is essential, for they have become a major force in the contemporary world. The top five hundred industrial corporations employ only 0.05% of the human population but control 70% of world trade, 80% of direct foreign investment, and 25% of world economic output. The sales of the largest companies, such as General Motors, Ford, Mitsui, Mitsubishi, Royal Dutch Shell, Exxon and Wal-Mart, exceed the GDP of dozens of countries, including Poland, Norway, Greece, Thailand, and Israel.

Wealth and power entail responsibility. If managers are truly responsible, they shift from a narrow shareholder-oriented philosophy to a broader stakeholder orientation. You should insist that they make this shift. But just what is involved in doing so?

The shareholder philosophy is decades old, put forward by Milton Friedman in an influential 1970 article in *The New York Times Magazine*. In this philosophy, management is merely the agent of the company's owners—its sole responsibility is to represent their interests, which means making profit for the shareholders. The concept of *stakeholders* was not widely known at the time. It grew to prominence later, when

45

Who Are the Stakeholders?

A company's stakeholders are those individuals, groups and organizations

- Who are affected by the company's activities—whether positively or negatively;
- Who provide some form of benefit or some kind of resources for the activities of the company;
- Who face some level of risk connected with the activities of the company; and
- Whose opposition or resistance to the company's activities creates a risk for the company itself.

Within the company, the stakeholders include employees, clients, customers, business partners, and investors (including the shareholders);

within the given industry the stakeholders include unions, regulators and competitors;

and within society at large they include host communities, local or national governments, civil organizations and, last but not least, individuals who, though neither clients nor customers, live in regions or are active in fields that are affected by the company's activities.

it became evident that corporations are a decisive factor in the life of the communities and countries where they operate.

You can promote the shift to a stakeholder philosophy by patronizing companies that embrace it, and boycotting or ignoring those that persist in the obsolete concept that the responsibility of business begins and ends with the short-term profit of the company's shareholders. You should insist that management—

- Accurately and honestly represents to the public the long-term benefits and costs of the company's products and services, including their safety, durability, social consequences, environmental toxicity, reusability and recyclability
- Consults its employees when formulating the goals and objectives of the enterprise
- Actively seeks to reduce pollution and environmental damage and minimize waste in the company's production processes, and throughout its supply and distribution chain
- Gives preference to ethical companies as partners and associates, and refuses to do business with companies that behave unfairly toward their employees, customers and the communities, or degrade the environment
- Takes an active interest in the lives of employees, discovering their concerns, understanding their needs, and contributing to their personal development
- Takes a similarly active interest in the people of the local communities, encouraging employees to devote part of their time to social work, or the improvement of the local environment

If you have the means, you can buy at least a few shares in a company and join one of the many newly created shareholders associations. You can then raise your voice in shareholder assemblies and use your vote—an effective way to get executives to provide full and honest accounts of corporate activities, and information on the real nature of the company's products and services.

Corporate responsibility for society and the environment is not charity; it is becoming a major factor of success in business. The public increasingly values responsible attitudes toward society and nature. A survey of more than 1,000 U.S. consumers in March 2001 and again in October 2001, reported in the *Harvard Business Review* of March 2002, showed a large increase in the importance people place on a company's behavior in regard to well-being in society.* It is not mere coincidence that the most publicized bankruptcies of recent times—Enron and K-Mart—involved companies that entirely lacked stakeholder responsibility. Enron was notorious for its greed and focus on short-term profit, and K-Mart came last on the Total Social Impact Foundation's ranking of the Standard & Poor 500 companies. Arthur Andersen and Worldcom were likewise noted for irresponsible and unethical practices. On the other hand, many of the companies who ranked high on the list of Best 100 Corporate Citizens are successful in the marketplace as well.

Interacting with the Commercial Media

There are further things we can and should do when it comes to the media. The flow of information in today's world is enormous, but it is seldom truly relevant to people's lives. In the case of commercial media, the market determines the information that reaches the public: people get what they are willing to buy. Believing that the public is interested in few things other than war, crime, sports, the stock market, and the views and doings of celebrities, the national and international commercial media concentrate on sensational items with "news value" and "human interest". But a daily diet of such items does not help you and me to make informed choices about the issues that decide our well-being and our prospects for the future.

---

* The question posed in the survey was, "I place importance on a company's support of charitable causes when I decide..."

...what to buy or where to shop
   pre-September 11: 52%
   post-September 11: 77%

...where to work
   pre-September 11: 48%
   post-September 11: 76%

...which companies to invest in
   pre-September 11: 40%
   post-September 11: 63%

...which companies I would like to see doing business in my community
   pre-September 11: 58%
   post-September 11: 80%.

The media could operate more responsibly, and we have the power to make them do so. We can select television and radio programs, internet sites, newspapers, magazines, and books that provide pertinent and constructive news, rather than merely sensational items. A number of alternative good news reports and newsletters are published by private non-governmental organizations. There is also a full-sized newspaper devoted to these issues, *Positive News*, published in England. Such publications are only now beginning to reach a critical mass in society. If more people would ask for them, we would soon find a page or a column in the national daily papers with relevant information, and more programs on radio and television. They would render an important service, informing people about cooperative communities, ethical movements, ways of sustainable living, efficient, environmentally friendly technologies, and non-polluting products, among other things. Asking for such news items to come on stream is not asking for charity: it is asking that the commercial media remain relevant to the concerns of the public. That, after all, is in their own interest.

Things We Can and Should Do in the Civic Sphere

Although business is more powerful than ever, the role of government remains decisive. There are problems of peace and security and public well-being to which only an enlightened political leadership can respond. If your government is not ready to do so, you can lift your voice and join with others in challenging its policies. To do so is to exercise the rights of *demos*, the people—an essential part of democracy.

As a concerned citizen, you can and should ask your government to—

- Take into account the changing lifestyles, patterns of consumption, values and expectations in the various cultures and subcultures of your society
- Adopt safer and more efficient technologies in public

services, especially in the energy, transport, and communication sectors
- Research, design and implement projects for healthier and more natural living in cities and towns
- Bring on line up-to-date complementary healing methods in public health care
- Make available ways and means for people to enjoy the natural environment without destroying ecological balances and despoiling or reducing wilderness areas
- Relate to the governments of other countries in a spirit of fairness, making full use of the available institutions and channels for peaceful and mutually beneficial intergovernmental cooperation

A good way to exercise your power in the civic sphere is to ask your elected representatives to take a "peace and sustainability pledge" to represent your best interests as a national and global citizen.

The Elected Representative's Peace and Sustainability Pledge

"I commit myself to:

- Make concrete progress toward peace, as well as social, economic, and ecological sustainability a top priority throughout my term in office;

- Analyze and assess all current and proposed legislation in view of whether or not it promotes peace and sustainability locally as well as internationally;

- Inform myself and my constituency, on the issues that are relevant to peace and sustainability in my state or district, as well as nationally and internationally."

You in turn should pledge to give your vote only to officials who take this pledge.

The responsibilities of the government include public education. In most parts of the world the educational system is outdated; it needs to be made more relevant and effective. It is up to the citizens of a democratic country to insist that their community and their state, and the federal administration itself, take effective steps to update and upgrade the school system.

In addition to the familiar tasks of creating an environment where children and young people can learn without discrimination and violence, there is a need to update the content and the form of public education. The content of education needs to include, in addition to the standard curriculum, classes, seminars, and informal discussion groups centered on current issues and problems, and ways young people themselves could contribute to public debate. Students need to be given the opportunity to confront such fundamental issues as peace and sustainability in their own community, as well as in their country and the world at large. They need to become acquainted with changes in values and beliefs in their own culture and society, as well as in other cultures and societies. They must be allowed to participate in the unfolding debate on alternatives to war and violence both locally and globally, and be given guidance in the search for ethical and responsible ways to live and to act.

Civic education is not complete until young people know how their community and country handle the burning issues of the times, and what they themselves can do about it. They must also know how they can interact with local businesses and the media in order to enhance sustainability and economic justice in their community.

The form of education must change in line with its content. There must be occasions when the young people do the talking and the teachers do not lecture but merely listen, and provide information when needed. On these occasions the students themselves define the agenda of the discussions and talk freely in small groups that include both boys and girls, and high as well as low achievers. Experience shows that opportunities to express themselves within the school curriculum are much valued by young people and produce lasting effect, leading to better understanding, cooperation, and solidarity in the school environment as well as beyond.

Harry Truman once said, "The buck stops here," meaning the desk of the president. Today the buck is more democratic: it stops with each and every one of us. *You* make the crucial difference between breakdown and breakthrough in society, in the economy, and in the local and global environment. You make this difference with the way you think and act. In today's world it is neither wealth and power, nor the control of territory and technology, that make the crucial difference. How you think and act shapes our present and decides our future. With responsible thinking and acting, you become part of the solution instead of remaining part of the problem.

✑ FIVE

A Star to Follow

A star on the firmament may seem like a far-out thing to envision, yet envisioning it is important. The importance of seeing a star is not the possibility of reaching it, but of having it before our eyes to guide our steps.

A good star for us to have is a positive vision of the world of the future. When we take the year 2020 for our dateline, the star has practical guidance value. For most young people today, a "vision 2020" could become reality.

Let us try an experiment in bold yet disciplined imagination. Let us imagine that we hear a young woman telling us how people think and live in 2020. And then, before getting back to the present, let us listen to a young man who completes her account by reporting on how the 2020 world is structured, and how it is organized.

Vision 2020: Reports from a Peaceful and Sustainable World

How We Think and How We Live
Values, Lifestyles and the New Consciousness

Report by a Young Community Counselor

The world in 2020 is in many respects similar to the world I knew as a young girl in the early years of this century. There are nearly 200 countries, some of them industrialized, others predominantly rural. Some of them make full use of the latest technologies, others prefer being guided by their traditions. There are two dozen giant cities, but they are not growing any bigger. Most people live in sustainable communities in medium-sized cities and towns and in rural environments. People are just as diverse as at the turn of the century, and since life is less stressful and more relaxed, cultural diversity can flourish without arbitrary constraints by hunger, joblessness, and heavy-handed bosses and governments. North Americans and Latin Americans, Japanese, Chinese, Indians and Asians, the same as Europeans, Africans, Australians and Polynesians, can express their values and safeguard their traditions.

Abject poverty has been all but eliminated: everyone's right to food, housing, education, and socially useful remunerated work is recognized and respected. We do not all live at the same material standard; some of us are more affluent than others. Yet the affluent among us do not use their wealth for ostentation and wasteful luxury. Even the comparatively rich adopt simple lifestyles, far simpler than those of rich people in the 20th century. They do so voluntarily—not just because legislation and taxes offer economic incentives, but because of a sense of responsibility for themselves, their neighbors, and their environment.

We do not believe that living well calls for amassing material goods. It means living comfortably, in some cases even luxuriously, but luxury does not lie in the quantity of the goods we own or control, but in achieving a high quality of lived experience. The dominant aspiration is personal rather than economic growth. It is the growth of intellectual and emotional life, achieved not in the isolation of a private dwelling, whether mansion or hut, but in the embrace of family, community and country, and the global community of all peoples and countries.

As we join together to improve the quality of the living and working environment, our community life enjoys a renaissance. There is a renaissance of spirituality as well. More and more women and men rediscover a higher and deeper dimension of their life. Since physical existence is now more assured, there is less pressure on people, and this leaves more time for family, community and nature, as well as for inner development.

People live longer and healthier lives, but the population of the world is not growing any further. Longer life-spans are offset by smaller families as people realize that it is irresponsible to produce children beyond the replacement level. This has obvious benefits. With a modest family size we are able to take better care of our children, ensuring that they grow into healthy individuals, with sufficient education to live peacefully and sustainably, in harmony with human society and with nature.

The New Consciousness

The changes we have wrought in the world are not the result of temporary trends and fads, nor do they obey the dictates of a higher authority. They result from the new mindset that emerged in my generation. This is a planetary consciousness, in some ways very different from the limited, ego-bound materialistic consciousness that dominated the world during my childhood in the early years of this century.

There are many things that differentiate the people of the Earth as we head into the third decade of the 21st century: religious beliefs, cultural heritage, economic and technological development, climate, and environment. Yet, notwithstanding our diversity, our new consciousness makes it possible for us to share some basic ideals.

As other people before us, we aim to achieve our own interests, yet we hope to achieve our interests consistently with the interests of all people whose interests are at stake.

We aim for democracy, yet for more than political democracy: we aim to ensure the best interests of all the citizens of our country.

It is our ideal to aim for fairness towards all people, but for more than fairness: for goodwill among peoples, nations, and cultures.

We aim for the rule of law, but for more than the means to enforce laws: to develop genuine respect for laws that protect the rights of individuals and states.

We also wish for economic success, but for more than the self-centered accumulation of riches: we aim to achieve conditions in which all people can enjoy an acceptable level of material well-being.

We aspire to social development, but to more than developed social structures and infrastructures: we wish to build a society that can ensure a high quality of life for all its people.

We ask for tolerance for different people and different cultures, but we wish to have more than mere tolerance: we aspire to find ways to actively pursue our shared interests, based on the unity that underlies our diversity.

We aim for freedom from oppression, hunger, and misery, but we strive for more than that: for the freedom to develop our own self and personality, through responsible lifestyles of our choosing.

We aim for humanism in all actions and decisions that affect other people, but our humanism is not abstract: it embraces the planetary ethic of living in a way that allows all people to live in conditions that permit material well-being as well as spiritual growth.

Last but not least, we aim for personal, corporate, and civic goals without sacrificing or impoverishing the environment, and we try to reach such goals with full regard for the right to life of all the things that live on this planet.

We have come to some new insights.

We know, and feel with every cell of our body, that all seven billion of us are inhabitants of Earth, with an equal right to enjoy its resources and its life-supporting environment.

We are convinced that it is immoral for any of us to live in a way that detracts from the chances of the rest of us to achieve a life of basic well-being and human dignity.

We believe that the universal rights adopted by our forebears in the 20th century—the right to freedom of expression, freedom to elect our leaders, and freedom from torture and other arbitrary constraints on personal liberty, as well as the right to food, shelter, education, and employment—that these rights apply to everyone in the global community, and deserve to be respected above and beyond considerations of personal, ethnic, and national self-interest.

We realize that it is more effective to exercise responsible trusteeship of the human and natural sources of wealth on this planet than to exploit them for narrow and short-term benefit.

We recognize that nature is not a mechanism to be engineered and exploited, but a living system that brought us into being, that nourishes us and, given our awesome powers of exploitation and destruction, is now entrusted to our care.

And we have learned that the way to solve our problems and conflicts is not by attacking each other, but by opening ourselves up to a dialogue that leads to a better understanding of each other, and to cooperating in ways that serve our joint interests.

How We Are Organized

Politics, Economics and Technology in the Post-Crisis World

Report by a Young School Teacher

The nations of this world are free to choose their preferred social structures and economic systems—ours is a world rich in diversity. Yet diversity does not spell conflict and disunity. We have not fragmented the human community into isolated units pursuing separate goals without regard for the common good. Our diverse nations and cultures are united by common values and aspirations, centered on creating a world where all people can live safely and peacefully, without destroying the life-sustaining environment.

It is a measure of our achievement that the fears that dominated the first decade of this century—fears of terrorism, armed conflict, economic breakdown, famine, ecological collapse, and invasion by destitute migrants—are behind us. Stability is the hallmark of our world—not the rigid stability imposed by a powerful authority, but the stability of a sustainably built network of self-reliant but cooperative communities, states, nations, and continental and sub-continental federations of nations.

Our System of Political Organization

The 20th century's system of self-centered nation states has been transformed into a transnational system, organized as a series of administrative and decision-making forums, with each forum having its own sphere of competence. This is not a hierarchy, for the forums at the various levels have considerable autonomy and are not subordinated to the higher levels. In the areas of peace and security, the protection of the environment, information and communication, as well as international finance, decision-making is global. But there is significant autonomy at local and regional levels. The world is a "heterarchy": a multilevel structure of distributed decision-making. It is aimed at combining global coordination with local, regional, and national autonomy.

Multiple links of communication and cooperation criss-cross our interlinked social, political and economic systems. Individuals jointly shape and develop their local communities. These communities participate in a wider network of cooperation that includes, but does not stop at, the level of nations. Nation-states in their turn are part of continental or sub-continental social and economic federations.

For linking the whole world we have the United Peoples' Organization, the body that succeeded the United Nations. The UPO observes, as do all other decision-making bodies of the world, the well-known but previously seldom respected "principle of subsidiarity". This means that decisions are made at the lowest level at which they are effective. The global level of the UPO, the world's highest level of decision making, is at the same time the lowest level at which peace and security can be effectively safeguarded, the world environment can be cared for, and the flow of money, technology, and information across the continents can be regulated. All other issues of public policy are the concern of communities, states, and federations at subsidiary levels of decision-making.

The UPO's political members are continental and sub-continental economic and social federations representing the shared interests of their member nations. They include the European Union, the North American Union, the Latin American Union, the North-African Middle-Eastern Union, the Sub-Saharan African Union, the Central Asian Union, the South and Southeast Asian Union, and the Australian-Nippon-Pacific Union.

The system of regional federations constitutes the Peacekeeping Council of the UPO, operating with a mandate similar to that of the former Security Council, but without the two-tier structure where some members are permanent and others not, and some have veto-power and others do not. The Peacekeeping Council commands the major military force in the world: the United Peacekeeping Force. The UPF is staffed by contingents from the member states of the federations. It undertakes peacekeeping missions at the request of the member federations.

The United Peoples' Organization is not uniquely a political organization: it has members also from civil society and business. Civil society members include various non-governmental organizations, active in social, economic and the environmental domains. Thanks to their membership, the voice of the international NGO community is no longer foreign to policy-making in the world; it is an integral part of deliberations and decisions in all the relevant areas.

The corporate membership of the Organization is made up of federations of businesses in the major branches of the private sector. Through specialized agencies in finance, industry, commerce, and labor, inherited from the United Nations and reformed in the light of the Organization's enlarged mandate, the UPO connects its member business federations with the representatives of the communities in which they operate. It helps managers establish good community relations, create mutually agreed codes of conduct, and reach mutually beneficial agreements on trade, employment, finance, and the protection of the environment.

Global-level coordination is a precondition of successfully restoring the viability of the environment, re-establishing natural balances in the composition of air, water, and soil, and preserving the integrity of the biosphere's regenerative cycles. Thus the World Environment Organization has been created as an affiliate of the UPO, to coordinate the environmental programs of the continental and sub-continental federations.

The continental and sub-continental level is effective for coordinating decision-making at the next subsidiary level: the level of nation-states. The economic and social federations provide a forum for the representatives of member nations to discuss their concerns, explore areas of mutual interest, and coordinate their political goals and social-economic practices.

The tasks and responsibilities of nation-states have not changed significantly. National governments remain the principal arbiters of their country's economic and social objectives. Nation-states maintain a national treasury, a national judicial system, police force, and health system. But these institutions do not operate under the premise of absolute sovereignty. Domestically they are integrated with the administrations of cities and rural areas, and internationally with the structures and policies of other states in the federation to which a given nation belongs.

The local level of coordination and decision-making serves cities, towns, and villages. At this level direct democracy is the rule. The representatives of the people respond directly to the people. The customary mechanism is the town hall meeting, held face to face whenever and wherever possible, and electronically when distance or cost prevents a significant number of people from participating.

Our System of Economic Organization

National economies seek their own balance between market forces, the valuation of natural assets, the environment, and social welfare. Some countries provide a guaranteed income for their people in order to assure their basic needs. Previously unpaid work, such as maintaining a household, caring for others and for the environment, and growing one's own food, is recognized to be socially and economically useful. In this way people in the majority of today's nation-states do not depend on competing in the market for staple food, shelter, and basic education. They can choose their preferred work or profession free of existential worries.

Achieving full sustainability in our economies is not utopian. With changed values and lifestyles came changed consumption patterns, resulting in lower energy and material requirements and more modest and efficient uses of energy and raw materials. Thanks to efficient resource use, less waste and simpler lifestyles, the size of the ecological footprint of cities and economies has dropped in all parts of the world. The size of the footprint of individuals is approaching the sustainable Earth-share: on the average it is not much above two hectares per person.

The world's monetary system has undergone much-needed reform at all levels—global, regional, as well as local. We no longer use U.S. dollars and Euros, national and continental currencies, as if they were global ones. The UPO issues a world currency, the Gaia, on the basis of the population of an economic and social federation rather than its economic strength. The federations have their own currencies, which they spend into circulation and take back through taxes. Their currencies are used for trade between a federation's member states; the Gaia is reserved for inter-federation transfers. As a result of such reforms even the least developed economies have overcome abject poverty, dependency and marginalization.

Business and politics are no longer at odds. Without dictates from above, the private sector is becoming a voluntary part of civil society. The aspiration of business managers is not solely the increase of shareholder value through a company-centered exploitation of all available resources, but to live up to the ethics of trusteeship of the shared wealth-producing assets.

Managers are concerned about assuring success for their companies, but like some business leaders in the 19th and early 20th century, they also seek a place among the builders of society. They endeavor to overcome the tension between efficiency, profitability, and dynamism on the one hand, and solidarity, equity, and sustainability on the other. They select the products and services they bring to the market in consultation with their clients and customers, as well as with their employees and partners. Even if production and marketing decisions are made with an eye towards success in the marketplace, they are informed also by regard for impact on the environment, employee satisfaction, and the human and social utility of the company's products and services. In consequence, much of the wastefulness of last century's throwaway culture is eliminated; built-in obsolescence has become obsolete in itself.

Technology is no longer valued for itself. We seek to make technology our servant rather than our master. Most of our technologies are more advanced than those of the early 21st century, but not all technologies that are available are actually put to use. Social utility and environmental friendliness are major factors in choosing which technologies to develop.

A major change in the use of technology occurred in the aftermath of the deepening conflicts and escalating wars of the first decade of the century. The leaders and peoples of the world realized that there are no reliable measures to prevent technologies intended for defense from being used for aggression, with disastrous consequences. Since it was not feasible to eliminate weapons of mass destruction from the arsenal of all states as long as any state possessed them, the members of the United Peoples Organization decreed worldwide disarmament, with implementation vested in the continental and sub-continental federations. In consequence, in the armaments field, research and development focuses not on producing more and more potent devices for killing and destruction, but on effective and reliable ways to verify that they are not being produced by any nation in the world.

There has been a corresponding de-escalation in the civic use of weapons. Criminality and violence are at a low level, thanks to improved social conditions and more balanced development in the economic sphere. With a lower level of frustration there is less resentment and hate, and the near-inaccessibility of lethal weapons reduces the incidence of gang-wars, massive killings and organized crime. There is no longer need for large, highly equipped police forces and high-security prisons. With the exception of special forces, law-enforcement officers are equipped much as 20th century English policemen were—with rubber sticks and handcuffs, now occasionally supplemented by temporarily disabling non-invasive lasers.

The most important advance in technological development is in the way we derive the energies we need. We have eliminated risky nuclear reactors and greatly reduced our use of fossil fuels. Nearly half of our energies come from the sun, as a direct source through photovoltaic and solar thermal technologies, and indirectly in the form of hydropower, wind, wave, tidal, geothermal and biomass-based energy. Our entry into the "solar age" not only brings a practically infinite source of energy without polluting air, land and water, but also helps re-balance the world's economy, since solar radiation reaches almost everywhere on the six continents, and is particularly intense in the tropical and sub-tropical regions where many of the less developed economies are concentrated.

In industrial production, current technologies produce what is needed and beneficial without creating eliminable side effects. There have been great improvements in recycling industrial and household wastes, and in eliminating by-products that pollute air, land, and water. The ultimate aim is to achieve zero waste.

In agriculture the emphasis is on maintaining biological diversity and producing a safe and sustainable supply of basic foods. We realize that the human body is part of terrestrial nature and natural foods are the best suited to maintaining its health and vigor. In addition to food production, agriculture is a source of natural energies and raw materials. Plants such as hemp grow prolifically almost everywhere, and they offer a renewable raw material for producing paper, textiles and oil, as well as some new varieties of plastics.

Much effort is devoted to ensuring a sustainable supply of clean water. A worldwide program to replant our forests has helped to reduce droughts and rebalance the climate. In arid coastal regions traditional sources are supplemented by desalinated seawater.

Our transport technologies aim at reconciling the requirement for mobility with the requirement for personal safety and public health. This is much less of a problem than it was at the turn of the century, for the emphasis on local self-reliance and autonomy reduced the need for people and goods to move long distances. The valuation of natural assets has been another factor: it made us aware that energy, even if renewable, is to be used with care, and that transport systems, even when ecological, have an unavoidable negative impact on nature. This impact is limited, but not totally eliminated, by the use of clean renewable energies, such as plant-based fuels, liquid hydrogen, electricity, fuel cells, compressed air, and various hybrid motive technologies adapted to local conditions and requirements.

The communication technologies in use today are highly advanced, but they are not substantially different from those of the early years of the century. Hardware is smaller, cheaper, and more powerful, and software is both simpler and more effective, adapted to use by people in all walks of life. Computers are at work in many facets of daily life and work. They eliminate some chores and make others easier, but they do not revolutionize our existence in the way technological forecasters and science fiction writers envisaged. We still live on Earth in human communities and the embrace of nature. We make use of technology to live better and more sustainably.

Advances in health-related technologies make a further contribution to our quality of life. Invasive medical procedures are limited to cases of birth defects, accidents, and serious malady. A softer and more holistic approach predominates in most other cases. The accent is on the maintenance of health through the prevention of disease, and this requires that we consider the human being as an integrated whole of body and mind, and an integral part of his or her society, culture, and environment.

The techniques that foster our inner development are an offshoot of our holistic approach to health. These "soft technologies" combine ancient methods with new biomedical and psychophysical methods. They are recognized adjuncts to human growth and development, and they are widespread and widely accepted.

People are still people, the Earth is still the Earth, but, as the young community counselor just told you, we have new thinking and a new consciousness. This has made the crucial difference. As the consciousness of individuals evolves, society reaches a new stage of maturity. It has a greater capacity for self-determination with more detachment and level-headedness; it is more inclusive, embracing people from differing ethnic groups, races and religions in a search for common ground; it is more anticipatory, assessing the merit of today's decisions in light of their effect on other people as well as on future generations, and it is more flexible, able to mobilize people's will and shared resources without waiting for crises to force last-minute responses.

Back to Earth: Getting Started

The alternative to a world beset by misery, conflict and violence is a world that is equitable and sustainable, and inspires peace in people's hearts. This is the kind of world we could build in the next few decades—*if we muster the will and the vision.*

Will we muster the will and the vision? The answer is not written in the stars, although having a star to follow is a useful, and even a necessary condition of achieving them. After all, we must know where we *can* go, if we want to decide where we *ought* to go. But once we have a good star and know where we should go, we must shift our gaze from the heavens to the earth—to the ground before our feet.

A Chinese proverb tells us that even a journey of a thousand miles begins with the first step. The journey before us is measured not in miles but in years, and we are not alone in setting out on it: we are joined by more than six billion fellow human beings. It is a crucial journey, taking us either to a more peaceful and sustainable world, or to conflict, violence, and chaos. We must take the first step—and it must be the right step.

If as a responsible global citizen your goals in life include an earnest desire to better the world, the first step is to look to yourself. It is no longer true that changing the world calls only for power and wealth—for dominating other peoples and cultures, and engineering nature. In our day changing the world calls also, and above all, for cultivating a non-technological and non-monetary yet effective and most precious resource: our consciousness. Addressing a joint session of the U.S. Congress, former Czech president Václav Havel warned, "Without a global revolution in the sphere of human consciousness, nothing will change for the better...and the catastrophe towards which this world is headed—the ecological, social, demographic, or general breakdown of civilization—will be unavoidable." Fortunately the inverse is also true: with a global revolution in the sphere of consciousness the catastrophe towards which the world is headed is avoidable. As Mikhail Gorbachev points out in his Introduction, if we become conscious that a turning in human affairs is truly necessary and decide to do what we can, together we can accomplish all that is necessary.

Many people still believe that there is a gulf between pragmatic policy-oriented solutions to the world's problems, and spiritual, human-growth-based solutions. This, however, is not true. The practical and the spiritual—the "outer" and the "inner"—approaches are inextricably linked. Changing the world is both a practical activity you need to pursue in the world at large, and a spiritual quest you must undertake directly within yourself. There is a need for active engagement with the great issues of our times as well as for inner growth; only if you have both can you take part in the spiritual/practical revolution that is the brightest hope for the human future.

In the next chapter Japanese spiritual teacher Masami Saionji makes clear that we can launch such a spiritual and at the same time practical revolution here and now, using the tools of our own mind. The aim is not to achieve enlightenment on a mountaintop, but to attain an evolved consciousness and focus it on the world we live in. The 20th century was littered with failed mass utopian movements. The challenge of the 21st is to channel the evolution of human consciousness into a movement that leads to fundamental social, political, and environmental healing.

The spiritual/practical movement that leads to a sustainable and peaceful world is not condemned to fail. It need not, and indeed must not fail; for it is the only feasible path to such a world. Happily, this path is already traveled by an impressive number of people. As the surveys of "cultural creatives" reviewed in Chapter 2 show, a growing number of Americans have entered on this path. They are developing more responsible ways of thinking and acting, and a more timely view of themselves and the world. They are evolving their values, their lifestyles, and their consciousness.

Evolving our consciousness is not something we do only for ourselves—it is something we do also for others...for all others, and for the Earth. Because when we open up and let our body and mind feel our ties with others and with nature, we change ourselves, and change others around us. When a sufficient number of people pray or meditate together, or find another path to evolve their consciousness, other people are affected as well. More sick people heal, divorce and suicide rates drop, crime and violence diminish. When many people open up, a powerful force develops—a leap of consciousness takes place. All the great prophets and sages of history knew this, Jesus as well as the Buddha, Mohammed as well as Zoroaster—and more recently Baha'ullah the same as Sri Aurobindo, Teilhard de Chardin and the Dalai Lama.

The evolution of our individual consciousness paves the way toward the evolution of our collective consciousness. This individual-collective evolution, more than anything else, can and must change this world.

MASAMI SAIONJI

SIX

You Can Change Yourself

BY MASAMI SAIONJI

All human beings, without exception, are continually creating themselves with the life-energy that is flowing within them. To create is your life's mission, and without it there would be no life. For better or worse, you continue to live because you continue to create.

What do you create? How do you create it? This is up to the free will of each of you.

What is your purpose in this world? I ask you this because at each moment your present self is created by the way in which you proceed toward this fundamental goal. As you progress toward this goal, from moment to moment you exert your creativity to create the self that you imagine yourself to be.

Create Yourself

The object of your creation is not a material object. Rather, it is your "self". It is your personality, your values, your habits, your future life. Material things always come second. As you continue to create and re-create yourself, the physical aspect

71

naturally follows. This is because the physical "you" is an extension of your essential, fundamental self.

However, if you forget that you are creating yourself and give all your attention to secondary things, misusing your shining creativity for attaining those things, you may indeed acquire what you seek. Yet in doing so you will bring unhappiness upon yourself, because your actions have gone against the universal flow.

Today almost all of humanity has become confused and drifted away from the natural order, bent on creating secondary things. As a result, we are walking along a very dangerous path, a path lined with fear, pain, and suffering.

Through the ages, we human beings have continued to create ourselves, and this process has not yet ended. It will continue for as long as we have our life's breath. Every human being is a creator: whatever our country, whatever our religion, whatever our culture, each of us is in the process of creating ourselves. Senior citizens, adults, children, newborn babies, people of faith, atheists, materialists—each of us is continually creating our own "self". This is our original mission and the reason why we were born on Earth.

But in the course of time humans strayed from their essential truth. The further we strayed, the more distressed we became. The more distressed we became, the further we strayed.

More and more people are beginning to realize this. We have come to a moment when humanity can change its course and create itself in a totally new, positive way. This new creation may be performed with great joy and expectation, unlike anything we have experienced in the past. The process of creating a new, expansive self will bring us untold bliss. If we choose to follow this road, each person will surely recognize the pointlessness of creating more negative thoughts, words, or emotions.

If all of humanity progressively creates itself based on harmonious truths, even our bodies will be able to evolve indefinitely. All human beings will elicit the power to heal themselves of illness and to overturn all difficulties. As we continue to create ourselves, the workings of our creativity may expand in amazing ways, allowing all things to evolve and come together in perfect harmony.

There is no need for you to struggle further along an agonizing path. You are now ready to create your life anew. The past has ended and vanished. As more and more people join together in creating only good, bright, wonderful and harmonious things, each individual and the whole of humanity will rise to new heights during the new millennium.

The Power of Creativity

No one wants to admit that the difficulties they now face are of their own making. Most may not even realize that this is the case. As a result, when things go wrong many people simply assume that it is because they are destined to go through life as failures. Whatever the task, they feel that they cannot possibly accomplish it as well as others. Day after day they say to themselves: "It is no use! Whatever I do, nothing turns out right. Everyone thinks that I am a failure—and they are right!"

People like this see themselves as clumsy and untalented, and they live in constant fear of failure. Even when they put forth their best efforts, they accuse themselves of not trying hard enough. Because they are convinced that no matter how hard they try, they can never hold a candle to others, much of what they do is based on a wish not to be pitied, not to be laughed at, not to be slighted, not to be made miserable. Over a long period of time, these people have steadily created images of themselves as failures—as people without creativity.

To these people I would like to say: How can you believe that you are without creativity? Your present way of life was created by you alone, and that in itself is proof of your creativity!

What is this power called creativity? It is the power of life itself. It is the power to make your thoughts appear in this world. Creativity is the power you exert to convert your imagination to reality. If, like the "failed self" described above, you think you are a failure, and constantly create images of failure in your mind, it only means that you are forging the mold for a "failed self" and projecting it into your future.

It is up to you to create what you wish to create. You create it by using your own life force—your creativity—as you move toward your chosen goals.

How important it is for each of us to set our own goals! Once you decide what kind of life you wish to lead, or what kind of person you wish to be, your creative power acts upon that wish and your life takes shape in this world.

What would you like to do? What would you like to become? Is it your wish to become a person who is devoted to your family, or to be loved and respected by others? Do you envision yourself as a giving person who can lend a hand to people in trouble? Perhaps you would like to be someone who serves your country and promotes harmony among nations, cultures, and religions. Or, perhaps you have a special job in mind. Perhaps you would like to become a business manager, or an artist, a doctor, a nurse, or a social worker. Perhaps you long to become a pilot, a police officer, an architect, a gardener, a banker, a chef, a scientist, or an inventor.

Whatever you aspire to is fine. Once you have set your goal, you can take your first step in that direction. Do not expect, however, that all your dreams will come true in a single day.

Let us imagine that you are a young girl or boy who longs to become a concert violinist. If you deeply wish to play the violin well, you must progress through various levels of study, practice, and training, so that by degrees your life-energy can work toward this goal.

At all times, your creative power is unleashed by your own consciousness. Just as birth and death are inseparably linked in the continuum of life, creativity and consciousness are joined together within the life power that flows to you from your life's source. As you strive to achieve your goal, you continue to create yourself from moment to moment.

In this process you may experience both pain and joy, times when you feel like quitting, times when you feel distressed, rebellious, injured, or inferior. There may be times when you face temptations, or times when you even compete with your friends.

Also, various kinds of circumstances may appear in your life. You may have to move because of your parents' work, or you may find that you and your teachers hold differing views. Other conditions such as your family situation, your finances, or the level of your own skill, might pose challenges. During these times it will be important to find the wisest way to exert your creativity. If you always hold your goal in your heart, you will be able to create the most suitable choices for reaching it, no matter what difficulties may appear.

Whatever our goal, each of us must ask ourselves: "What do I need to do now? What should take priority in my thinking? With what sentiments will I respond to things?" There are many things to consider. To achieve a long-range goal, we must create smaller goals day by day and make choices from moment to moment.

To achieve the best results, we must never take a weak-spirited attitude under any circumstances. We must never give up hope.

Never Doubt Yourself

Until now, many people have been developing their lives in a negative direction. Rather than exerting their creative power to draw out their own marvelous capabilities, they have been using it to lean on others. When a task seems troublesome, they expend considerable energy finding ways to have it done by others. When a task seems demanding or challenging, they pour tremendous energy into relying on the talents of others. How to use others, how to hide behind others, how to avoid being despised, badmouthed, or laughed at by others: through long years of directing our creativity into efforts like these, we have become adept at the art of dependence. Very adept indeed.

How vexing it is to see this, when we know that, essentially, we are meant to use our creative energy for standing up on our own, developing our own talents, and walking along our own paths! All too often, people are either neglecting jobs that they are responsible for doing, or else hesitating to do things that they could be doing, simply because they are in the habit of depending on others.

How can we rise above a negative way of living? First and foremost, we must put an end to self-doubt. Believing in ourselves is our first step—our point of departure.

All those who lead unhappy lives are people who doubt themselves. All those who lead happy lives are people who believe in themselves. To believe in oneself is to live with dignity, confidence, and courage.

Why do people doubt themselves? It is because they do not truly know themselves, and are not actively trying to know themselves. If you really wish to be happy, sever your fondness for doubt. Doubt cannot create anything bright or new. Doubt only destroys. Doubt only attracts darkness. If doubt creeps into your mind, never allow it to run about uncontrolled. Confront your doubt immediately, and confirm whether it is rooted in reality. Once you know the facts, you can turn your attention toward the positive.

Above all, never doubt any member of your family. Whatever may happen and however things may look, let no trace of doubt appear. Doubt is strictly taboo. When you harbor no doubts, everything naturally moves toward the positive. Everything changes for the better.

The important thing is to cherish your heartfelt goal and hold it close to you each day. As the saying goes, many drops of water make a river. Little by little, what you create each day will grow into something bigger, until you accomplish your purpose in this world.

From beginning to end, life is a process of creation. The moment we die, the results of this process become clear.

There is no need to create anything grand at the beginning, but it is important to set your sights high. As you continue to create yourself, you can be sure that what you are aiming for will appear.

How happy we are to be able to create something wonderful. And where will it all lead?

The future is waiting to be created.

The Power of Your Words

Even one little word from us can hurt people's feelings or make them angry. And the reverse is also true: just one word from us can make people happy, or ease the pain that they feel.

Originally, though, this was not the purpose of words. Words were not developed so that people could speak to others, or exchange their ideas and feelings. The original purpose of words was different from this.

If this is the case, what is a word? Where does it come from, and what does it do? Is there not something extremely mysterious and significant about a "word"?

In reading ancient holy books, we sometimes feel mystified by phrases that bring up the idea of "word". We want to know more about it. We want to understand it. And so we ask questions.

In his work *Questions of Faith*, Masahisa Goi replied to one such question:

> *Question:* In the New Testament there is a verse which reads: *In the beginning was the Word...* (Jn 1:1). I feel that this verse must surely hold a high and precious truth, but I cannot catch hold of its meaning. Could you explain it to me?
>
> *Answer:* Generally speaking, when people think of a word they are simply thinking of an utterance produced through the oscillation of the vocal cords. However, when Jesus says "Word" he is referring to the reverberations, or waves, emitting from the source of the great universe. He is referring to waves of divine light. The same concept is also taught in the Shinto faith.

When divine light is conveyed by means of the physical voice, we also call it a "word". These light waves hold the power which creates everything in the universe... That is why we say that everything is composed of "words".[1]

Here is the way I understand it:

In the far distant past, when human spirits first branched out from their source, they were at one with the universe and could directly feel the resonance, or "word", issuing from the universal source. At the same time, they could naturally sense the feelings and intentions of others. To communicate with each other there was no need for them to use words. They could understand each other perfectly without any words, simply by sensing each other's ideas and feelings.

Even today, we can still witness this kind of unspoken, heart-to-heart communication. Mothers can perceive the feelings of their newborn babies or children too young to speak. Couples and family members can understand each other perfectly without any need for words. Through the thoughts and feelings that precede all words, people can naturally tune in to each other.

Why then, did we begin to use words? We began to use words, not to speak to others, but to speak to ourselves. When we felt a divine resonance issuing from higher-dimensional planes, we used words to speak about it to ourselves—not to others.

Yet what function did this serve? What was the need for words? People needed words to give form to matter in this three-dimensional world. We used words to enact material creation, through the superb wisdom, intuition, freedom, and creative power given to human beings. In rapid succession, material things were created through the spiritual power and divine energy of our awesome, mighty words.

Originally, the words that we spoke were addressed to ourselves and were simultaneously offered to the universal source. This resulted in people's individual energy, light, and power becoming concentrated and merging with the immense power from the universal source. This is what caused our thoughts to take shape as matter in this world. Nowadays, we call these kinds of activities "invention" and "discovery". They come about when we call forth our inner, creative power and manifest it through words.

Material creation cannot be drawn into this world through thoughts alone. Only when our thoughts are concentrated into "words", and have universal power and energy added to them, does matter take shape in this world. This is why I say that, in the original sense, words were not intended as a means of communication among people.

By exerting the remarkable wisdom, intuition, and creative power that exist within us, we human beings have created brilliant things, wonderful things, useful things, and things of beauty. We have found supreme delight in using our abilities to create the items that seemed most necessary, important, and valuable for humanity.

First of all, each of us figured out what was necessary for ourselves and for others. Then we expressed those ideas through "words" (concentrated energy), which we addressed both to ourselves and to the universal source. Through those "words", people cooperated with the infinite energy overflowing from the universal source and caused matter to manifest itself in this world.

In the beginning, humanity was in complete oneness with everything that existed in universal space. We were individual rays of life, subtle vibrations issuing from the one, all-inclusive *Life*. Then, at a given time, the universe gave birth to the human physical body by causing those subtle vibrations to attain a coarser, tangible frequency.

At first, because the vibrations of the physical human body had not become entirely coarse and tangible, as they are now, people could freely regulate their own vibrations. We could manifest our divinity by emitting delicate vibrations of light. Or, by making our vibrations coarser, we could become physical entities again. In this way, spirits could freely move back and forth through universal space, enjoying both our divine existence and our lives as human beings.

Then, little by little, people displayed increasing interest in the physical aspect of their lives. We began to feel that we would like to live in the physical plane for a longer period of time. To make a prolonged stay possible, it became necessary for us to exert our ingenuity to discover and invent new things. As individuals pooled their wisdom and made more and more innovations, we created the things necessary to prolong the life of our physical bodies. Through "words", we created material things one after another, and steeped ourselves in the delight of creation.

We also began to take an interest in things that other people had invented. The desire arose to make better, more useful, more amazing things—things that would startle and impress people. In this way human beings gradually began to compete with one another.

At first, people had a good and useful influence on each other. We stimulated and encouraged each other, and through this friendly competition we freely created marvelous, practical things. Then, bit by bit, this competitive spirit gained impetus, and the egoistic self took shape. Human interaction grew brisker and sharper, and eventually people directed their attention toward producing things which affected one another unfavorably.

The Laws of Harmony

Originally, human beings resided in a high-dimensional, heavenly kind of world. Then the situation gradually changed. The words people spoke caused injury, pain, and anger. Human consciousness was sinking to a lower level.

Meanwhile, human beings continued to create the things that they wanted to create. However, because the creation of harmful things went against the laws of harmony, the universal source refrained from providing the amount of energy that would be sufficient to manifest those things quickly. As a result, it began to take a very long time for matter to be created in this world.

As time went on, we human beings deviated more and more from our original truth, until we almost wholly detached ourselves from the divine intention. We no longer knew how to receive and utilize the energy that flows from the universal source.

As our interest in a materially-oriented life increased, we gathered up our capabilities and exerted them extensively. To be sure, this has resulted in an awesome development of material civilization, and some came to enjoy a life of material luxury. Yet in this process, we forgot the truth and light of our original being. For many long years it has remained dormant within us.

Even so, light and truth have never left human beings. Truth always lives firmly within each one of us. However, the ability to fully use our intrinsic wisdom, intuition, and healing power has been neglected. People's awareness has dropped to a lower dimension.

When light-filled thoughts are emitted, they turn into light-filled words, light-filled words induce light-filled creation, and light-filled creation produces light-filled matter. Because this process follows the universal law, it puts the energy of the universe into motion, making it possible for us to manifest brilliant, noble objects that are useful to humanity.

On the other hand, when the process takes a negative turn, negative thoughts lead to negative words, negative acts of creation, and negative matter—which runs counter to the law of the universe.

Thoughts and words are, in themselves, power. Therefore, negative thoughts and words create distorted matter, harmful phenomena, and adverse conditions. However, if additional energy is not supplied from the universal source, it becomes extremely difficult and takes an interminably long time for the manifestation process to complete itself. This, too, is nothing short of a great gift of love from the universe.

81

Consequently, even though we human beings have been sending out negative thoughts and words with all our might, negative materialization has, happily, been held down to the barest minimum. On the other hand, since it is so difficult for matter to be materialized in this world through negative words, our negative thoughts continue to circulate within us and, invigorated by the life energy that we give them, they end up wielding a strong influence on our minds and bodies. Also, since the negative words generated by our negative thoughts were originally directed toward ourselves, without realizing it we have been causing ourselves great pain and anguish, because all that we emit comes back to us. This is a law of creation.

Meanwhile, because we had formed a habit of directing our words toward others as well as toward ourselves, words came to be used in a way quite contrary to what was intended. As a result, the majority of people today think that words are mere tools for communication.

Because they think this way, people see nothing amiss in speaking malevolent words, cruel words, or words that bring pain to others. Nowadays, people wave their words like swords, fiercely assaulting others. They do not realize that those very words will eventually return to themselves.

To put it plainly, the process works like this: whatever we think and say, we think and say about ourselves. The moment the words leave our lips, we have spoken them to ourselves.

How scary that is! When we know that all our words are directed to ourselves, we begin to weigh our words and choose them carefully. We feel the need to use only good words that sparkle with light. Whatever the situation, we intentionally refrain from using negative, hateful, ominous words. We cannot bring ourselves to use them when we know that we are using them on ourselves.

But what have we been doing for such a long time? Since ages past, each human being has been turning the truth inside out. We have not been "using" words, but "abusing" words.

82

This terrible misuse of words has been the basis of the cold, cruel world that we have built around us.

As we progress through the 21st century, our illusions about words must be swept away. All negative words must be purified. If life on Earth is to keep evolving, all our words must become bright and harmonious.

Looking back on the history of humanity, we realize that it is because of the way in which each individual has been using words—and for no other reason—that we have had so much conflict, calamity, disease, and discrimination. Wars, diseases, natural disasters—all these things have come to humanity through the power of each person's spoken words.

If we wish to draw bright, harmonious conditions into this world, the best thing we can do is to think only good thoughts in our minds and speak only good words with our voices. We must give expression to our brightest hopes and wishes. We must say: *I can do it, for sure. Everything is possible. Everything will come together perfectly. Everything will change for the better. All ills will be resolved. All needs will be filled. Everything will find harmony. I will develop my talents. I will build wonderful friendships. I will have a splendid marriage...* We must give voice to our most cherished aspirations.

The words we speak are creating the world of the twenty-first century. As we continue to speak words filled with gratitude, praise, hope and encouragement, our words will attract the corresponding energy from the universe, producing conditions of health, happiness, harmony and limitless development in our future.

All living beings long to be soothed and enlivened by words filled with joy and light. All of humanity longs to melt into oneness with everything in nature and creation. This will come about when we respect all forms of life and shower them with words of praise and appreciation: *Thank you, beloved Earth! Thank you, air, water, mountains, oceans, rivers, stones, animals and plants!*

In the ultimate sense, "word" essentially means "vibration of life". All human beings and all living things are constantly sending out vibrations of life, or "words". The problem is that most of us do not hear those words. Or, it might be more to the point to say that we have lost our willingness to hear them. If only we would listen to those words, we would surely be able to hear them.

The rocks and the sand are speaking "words". The sea and the rivers are also speaking. Animals and plants are speaking. The sun, the stars and the planets are always speaking words—singing the praises of life—singing of the joy and the eternity of life.

Many people today have forgotten how to listen to those "words", but a time will surely come when all of us will re-awaken to them. At that time, nature will come alive again and harmony will spread throughout the Earth.

How You Can Invite Happiness

Which came first, the chicken or the egg? Everyone has heard this age-old question, and we could debate it at great length without ever finding an answer.

Let us suppose that the egg existed first, and later became a hen. We are then left with the riddle of where the egg came from in the first place. Inevitably, we have to conclude that the egg was born of the hen. The hen, however, was born from the egg. Thus the cycle of cause and effect continues endlessly— no one knows where it truly begins or ends.

For the moment, let us define the egg as the cause and the hen as the effect. One person might say that the cause (the egg) came first, while another might say that the effect (the hen) preceded the cause. Depending on your outlook and way of thinking, you could subscribe either to the theory of *cause and effect* or to the theory of *effect and cause*. It seems to me that everyone is free to choose either of them.

At this point, you might be saying that you know about the theory of cause and effect, but have never heard of the theory of effect and cause. That is because the theory of effect and cause is a new term, invented by me. Under the law of cause and effect, there is first a cause, which is followed by an effect. With the law of effect and cause, there is first an effect, which in turn produces a new cause.

What is my reason for introducing this concept? For a long time, people have been placing heavy restrictions on themselves on account of cycles of cause and effect that have continued since past ages. It pains my heart to see their anguish, and I wish to help them set themselves free, so they might live happy and creative lives.

THE LAW OF CAUSE AND EFFECT—If you sow violet seeds in the ground, violets will grow and bloom. Here, the planting of the seeds is the cause. It precedes its effect, the blooming of violets.

Because the couple fell in love, they married. ...Because the mother-in-law always bullied her daughter-in-law, the daughter-in-law came to dislike her. ...Because the husband was unfaithful, the marriage ended in divorce. In these examples, we again recognize certain causes as producing certain effects. All the circumstances in the world can be explained through the law of cause and effect. This law is widely known and accepted in today's world.

Yet if human beings thoroughly understand the law of cause and effect, why do they keep re-enacting the same miseries and failures? If they recognize that their present pain and sadness are the results of past causes, why do they not vow never again to repeat those same failures?

The law of cause and effect offers us a great key for identifying the causes of our unhappiness. However, if we never release ourselves from those past causes it will be extremely difficult for us to create happy futures.

THE LAW OF EFFECT AND CAUSE—Under the law of cause and effect, the cause of unhappiness always stems from a finite or relative view of the world. For example, people tend to think: "If only I had assets!" "If only I had a house or land!" "If only I were younger or more beautiful!" "If only I had better

85

academic credentials, or worked for a more prestigious company, or came from a better background!" There is no end to the list of things that people yearn for. For as long as people think in this way, it is inevitable that some will find happiness while others are relegated to unhappy situations.

The law of effect and cause, however, begins where we transcend the causes of a finite world. Under this law, we first generate a shining effect, so that a joyful new cause naturally follows. We begin by calling forth an effect from within the limitless realm of our creativity. Rather than focusing on the finite goals of a materially-oriented world, we turn our attention to the infinite possibilities of the spirit.

Actually, it is much easier to start by generating an effect of our own choosing. This is because such effects exist plentifully within us. Each person's imagination holds an unlimited source of love, health, and happiness. When we attune our consciousness to these immeasurable qualities, they will spontaneously generate a new set of causes.

Try thinking of the happy person who already exists within you. Let yourself imagine a feeling of continual harmony, calm, and peace of mind. Envision a cheery family where you are surrounded by your wonderful spouse and children. Picture yourself as you truly are in essence: radiant with vitality, living in tune with the universe.

Happiness is first awakened in the heart. Then, through the energy called forth from the heart, everything that causes happiness is drawn toward you. Even material happiness and happy human relationships will begin heading spontaneously in your direction.

This is the point I would like to emphasize: once you have understood the causes belonging to the material world, there is no need to be held down by them. Your next step is to look to the future. When you direct your attention to the limitless world of the spirit, the phenomena that you desire will naturally take shape in your life. Rather than defining your happiness in terms of the quantity of material benefits, say to

86

yourself that everything you desire already exists in a world that far surpasses the material one.

There is no need to live in constant fear of the law of cause and effect. Once a seed has been sown, you cannot remedy the situation by worrying about it. If you always live dreading the effects of your past actions, you will spend your days in fear and apprehension.

When the effects of your past actions emerge in your life, try thinking that all those things appear only in order to vanish forever. Do not be held down by the mistakes of the past. Continue to live brightly and confidently, in the firm belief that when those past causes have disappeared, things will definitely get better.

My theory of effect and cause goes one step beyond the law of cause and effect. It is a philosophy of steadfast, light oriented thinking which enables us to focus on what is bright. It is a way to call forth our unlimited potential. Happily, the way to do it is simple: when a dark thought crosses your mind, counter it with a bright one. When a pessimistic feeling surrounds you, pierce it through with the positive energy of an optimistic word. From morning till night, create shining new *effects*. In other words, create thoughts filled with harmony, happiness, optimism, and humanitarian love.

If, instead, you become wholly engrossed in tracking down the causes of each and every occurrence in your life, or each and every problem in the world, and try to analyze it according to the law of cause and effect, your efforts may never reach a conclusion.

Let me give you a simple example of what I mean: A man is not happy (effect). Why is he not happy? As a child, he was not loved by his mother (cause). Next, we ask why he was not loved (effect). It was because he was a rebellious child (cause). Why was he rebellious (effect)? It was because his mother ignored him in favor of her other children (cause). Why did his mother ignore him while showering affection on her other children (effect)? It was because, unlike her other children, he had a gloomy disposition (cause). Why was he gloomy as a child (effect)? It was because he was not given the things he wished to have (cause). Why was he not given the things he wished to have (effect)? It was because his family was short of funds (cause). Why was his family short of funds (effect)? And so on.

As we can see from this one example, researching the causes of our circumstances is a never-ending process. However far back we might go, we can never truly identify one single, original cause for an occurrence.

If we traced the matter back to the person's infancy, and tried to discover why he was born in those circumstances, we would have to trace his existence even further back, to a time before he was born in this world. But even if we were able to do so, we would still not be able to isolate any single cause behind his misfortune. And when it comes to the conditions among nations, the causes become even more complex. Behind every world problem there is always a complex interweaving of historical, cultural, social, economic and emotional causes. It is not a question of a single cause bringing about a single effect.

To the extent that we can, it may indeed be valuable to understand the causes behind a given situation. That in itself, however, may not point the way to a bright and happy future.

True Awakening

Each day, as I observe the confusion in people's hearts, I long to help disentangle it as much as I can. This is why I urge everyone to rediscover their intrinsic truth at the earliest possible moment.

Strangely enough, the moment of awakening occurs unexpectedly, in the space of an instant. True awakening is not the product of long-term effort, patience, or study, nor does it come with acquired knowledge. As long as you try to discover it through knowledge, it stays out of your reach.

What do I mean by "true awakening?" I mean the recovery of lost intuition—the universal wisdom given to each human being. Human beings still continue to wander about in confusion, shouldering needless burdens, because they are using only their limited knowledge without drawing on their reservoir of inner wisdom.

Your own intuitive perception is crystal clear. Now, at this moment, attune your heart to your flawless intuition, which comprehends everything. At this very moment it can sense what you need, what you must do, and where you should direct your steps as you walk along today's path.

Even if you could call forth every particle of knowledge that you have ever accumulated, it would not enable you to resolve the difficulties that presently stand before you. However considerable it might be, your knowledge pertains to your past experiences. It does not belong to the "you" who exists today. It cannot point out your direction for the future. While it might provide assistance in a minor way, it cannot offer you a fundamental solution.

From ancient times until today, how many people have lived out their lives relying only on stored knowledge? What legacy has it left us with? The answer is plain for anyone to see. It has given us war after war, illness after illness, famines, disasters, and all manner of suffering.

At long last, we have come to the moment when each member of the human family must make a fresh start and look toward the future. It is time for people to adopt new thinking.

If we really wish to be happy, if we really wish to be healthy and successful, the way to do it is to constantly focus our thoughts on the qualities and situations that we wish to draw out: overflowing happiness, shining health, fulfillment, harmony, friendship, prosperity, and gratitude toward everything in nature and creation.

By continuing to direct our consciousness toward the bright world of our cherished hopes and dreams, we will draw out the effects that lead to luminous future conditions. The happy situations that we envision will naturally take shape around us, and the wonderful people, things, talents, and insights that we desire will indeed come to us.

As more and more of us continue living in this way, with an unshakable belief in its effectiveness, we will soon discover that we have undergone a marvelous, inner change. By producing this change in ourselves, we shall indeed change the world.

May Peace Prevail on Earth—A Call to Action

As I look around this world, filled with tragedy and violence, my heart goes out to the young people of today. On behalf of my generation I wish to apologize to these young people, who must carry on in our place during the 21st century. It was our responsibility to pass on to you a peaceful world and a good, pure environment—a world in which all living things can exist in joy and harmony. However, we have not been able to carry out this responsibility. Instead, we created a world filled with violence, war, discrimination, poverty, disease, and environmental pollution.

Moreover our generation has used up an enormous part of the world's natural resources, even reaching into your share. Having inherited this difficult situation from us, how hard it must be for you to guide this world to peace and happiness. With all my heart I most sincerely do apologize.

I was born in Japan, during the Second World War. Like so many others, I lost relatives and loved ones through the violence of war. As you know, Japan is the only country to have experienced the devastation of the atomic bomb. And when all is said and done, there is one thing I am proud of. After the war was over, I never heard any of my countrymen express a desire for revenge.

After experiencing the tragedy of war, the Japanese people rejected war. Now we yearn more and more for peace. I would like to tell everyone how proud we are of our Peace Constitution, which says that Japan will not make or use weapons. We adopted this Constitution so that future generations might never experience war again, never experience

90

hatred again, and never create enemies again, but build a better life for themselves and their children.

My parents and grandparents had their fill of war. They learned that war cannot create anything beautiful and new. War only kills and destroys. It only affirms suffering and misery. And so, on behalf of theirs and my generation, I would like to say: Do not copy our past mistakes! There is no need for you to imitate our errors. Create your own future, a future that is totally bright and new.

In past generations we produced many kinds of violence: the violence of war and oppression, the violence of rape and child abuse, discrimination, intimidation, and environmental destruction. Until now, society has tried to quell these various kinds of violence with more violence. We have even taken pride in these efforts using terms like "the fight against disease", "the fight against poverty", "the fight against discrimination", "the war on crime", and now, "the war on terrorism".

Yet after pouring so much energy into fighting against violence, what has been the result? Even one look at today's world situation should give us the answer. Violence cannot bring an end to violence. It may briefly suppress it at a particular time and place, but in the end, fighting against violence only adds fuel to violence. Sooner or later it erupts again, even more forcefully.

For many people, the threat of terrorism is the most fearful kind of violence. Do you know the cause of terrorism? Is it poverty? Is it religion? Is it a lack of education? The more we think about it, the more we see that there is no one, single cause of terrorism. Rather, it occurs through the complex interaction of numerous historical, cultural, economic, political, religious, and social factors. And when we look even more deeply into the source of terrorism and violence, we find that its motivation springs from violent emotions that are boiling in each person's heart: anger, blame, resentment, humiliation, and self-hate. Yes, self-hate, self-blame and self-judgement, resulting from a loss of trust in the inner wisdom that speaks to us through the voice of our intuition.

People who trust themselves, and trust their intuition, can always forgive themselves. Even when they have made a mistake, or committed an act of violence, they can rise above it. They can say to themselves: What I did was wrong! I won't do that again! Starting right now I am going to make up for it. From this day forward I will love others and work for others!

But people who do not trust themselves cannot forgive themselves. They always blame, judge, and torment themselves. Then they seek relief by projecting some of that self-hate on others. When each and every human being is able to truly love himself, or truly understand and trust herself, no one will ever hate others or feel a desire for revenge.

After the Second World War, my adoptive father, Masahisa Goi, was inspired to start a revolution—a revolution in the human consciousness. And so he created these words: *May Peace Prevail on Earth*. Now, fifty years later, these words can be seen by people all over the world on tall poles called "peace poles". Have you ever seen a peace pole? Right now, there are more than 200,000 of them, standing in schoolyards, parks, public squares and private gardens all over the world. You may have seen some of them on television, in places like Sarajevo, Israel, Palestine, and Afghanistan. Peace poles have been welcomed by spiritual leaders such as the Dalai Lama, Mother Theresa, and Pope John Paul II, as well as by groups such as the Rotary Club. Some of you might feel that you would like to place a peace pole in your neighborhood, or at your school. But perhaps you are thinking: "I would like to, but I am too young. I am still a student. I don't know much. I have not had as much experience as other people." However, I can tell you: Peace is not born from experience. Experience can be a valuable teacher, but experience itself does not give birth to peace.

Peace is not born from education either. Education, like experience, can be a helpful aid, but it does not supplant the incredibly deep, intuitive wisdom that you hold within you.

What, then, gives birth to peace? The answer is simple. It is love, pure humanitarian love, sustained by courage, sincerity,

effort, optimism, and overflowing hopes for the future. For me, this spirit of love is expressed through a peace pole.

If you would like to put up a peace pole, what should you keep in mind? To me, the important thing is not to place peace poles only at famous or historical places, or only at places where tragedies have occurred, or only at places where a lot of people go. The important thing is to see peace poles *everywhere:* at places where many people go or where just a few people go—on street corners, in private gardens, in parks, in front of libraries, houses, shops, parking lots, restaurants, hotels,

apartment buildings, zoos, hospitals—any place where someone might see them. If you wished to, you might even place a
peace pole in a spot where people seldom go, such as in a for-
est or mountainous area, as a gift of gratitude to nature.

How can you choose a place for putting up a peace pole?
Just trust your intuition. Trust the clear, sparkling feeling that
naturally rises up within you. Then try. The more you try, the
more clearly your path will open up in front of you.

For many years I have had a very special hope, a very special dream. My dream is that someday, there may be many millions of peace poles: in all neighborhoods, in all regions, in all
countries and languages of the world. Every day, wherever a
person goes, I would like them to be able to see at least one
peace pole. I would like the sight of a peace pole to be more
familiar than the sight of a Coca-Cola sign, or a McDonald's!
I would like the words *May Peace Prevail on Earth* to resonate
in all people's hearts. I know that it is possible. We can make it
happen. It is already starting to happen.

In the 21st century, what creates peace is not governments,
or religions, or nations, or individual leaders. What creates
peace is *you*. Through your bright hopes, your efforts, and your
belief in peace, you can create peace and harmony for yourself,
your family, your country, your environment, and the world.

NOTE
1. *Questions of Faith*, Masahisa Goi, November 1959. English publication
   pending. Masahisa Goi (1916–1980) was a Japanese author and philosopher. His vision for peace was the inspiration for the Goi Peace
   Foundation, chaired by Masami Saionji.

PAOLO COELHO

The Tale of the Ancient Alchemists

BY PAOLO COELHO

A new way of thinking has become the necessary condition for responsible living and acting, says Ervin Laszlo in this book. And even if in one or another moment it may seem pessimistic, You Can Change the World, *in fact, echoes what many people in many parts of the world are already committed to achieve. It puts in place an important pillar for building a sustainable and peaceful world.*

Changing yourself and the world is like a great bicycle race whose goal is to accomplish the Personal Legend. According to ancient alchemists, that is our true mission on Earth.

At the start of the race we are together, sharing companionship and enthusiasm. But as the race goes on, the initial joy gives way to the real challenges: fatigue, monotony, doubt about one's own ability. We notice that some friends have already given up at the bottom of their hearts. They are still racing but only because they cannot stop in the middle of the route. This group gradually gets bigger. They all pedal alongside the support car, also known as Routine, talking among themselves and fulfilling their obligations, but they have forgotten the beauties and challenges of the journey.

Eventually we leave them behind. Then we are forced to face solitude, the surprise of unknown bends, problems with the bicycle. There comes a time, after a few falls with no one around to help us, when we ask ourselves if all the effort is worth while. Yes, it is worth while.

The point is not to give up. Rev. Alan Jones says our soul will be able to overcome all these obstacles if we can draw on Four Invisible Forces: love, death, power, and time.

It is necessary to love, because we are loved by God.

It is necessary to be aware of death, in order to understand life.

It is necessary to struggle for growth, but not to be fooled by the power that comes with growth, because we know it is worthless.

Lastly, it is necessary to accept that although our soul is eternal, at this moment it is caught in the web of time, with its opportunities and limitations. Thus in our solitary bicycle race we have to act as if time existed, to make the most of each second, rest when necessary, but continue traveling on toward the Divine light without allowing occasional anguish to defeat us.

These Four Forces cannot be treated as problems to be resolved, since they are beyond our control. We must accept them and let them teach us what we need to learn.

We live in a Universe that is both gigantic enough to include us and small enough to fit in our heart. The soul of man contains the soul of the world, the silence of wisdom. While we are pedaling toward our goal, it is always important to ask: "What is beautiful about today?" The sun may be shining, but if it is raining we should remember that the storm clouds will soon go away. The sky clears, and there is the sun as ever. It never passes. It is important to remember this at times of loneliness.

When things are very hard, we should not forget that everyone has felt this despair regardless of race, color, social condition, belief or culture. A beautiful prayer of Sufi master Dhu'l Nun the Egyptian (+ 861 AD) sums up the positive attitude required at such times:

O God, when I pay attention to the voices of animals, the sound of trees, the murmuring of water, the twittering of birds, the rush of the wind or the clap of thunder, I realize they bear witness to Thy unity. I feel Thou art the supreme power, omniscience, supreme wisdom, supreme justice.

O God, I recognize Thee in the ordeals to which I am subjected. Allow Thy satisfaction to be my satisfaction. May I be Thy joy, the joy a father feels for a child. And let me remember Thee with serenity and determination, even when it is hard to say that I love Thee.

✧

THE CLUB OF BUDAPEST'S

Manifesto on Planetary Consciousness

A new way of thinking has become the necessary condition for responsible living and acting. Evolving it means fostering creativity in all people, in all parts of the world. Creativity is not a genetic but a cultural endowment of human beings. Culture and society change fast, but genes change slowly. No more than one half of one percent of the human genetic endowment is likely to alter in a century, and hence most of our genes date from the Stone Age or before. They could help us to live in the jungles of nature, but not in the jungles of civilization. Today's economic, social, and technological environment is our own creation, and only the creativity of our minds—our culture, spirit, and consciousness—will enable us to cope with it. Genuine creativity does not remain paralyzed when faced with unusual and unexpected problems but confronts them openly, without prejudice. Cultivating such creativity is a precondition of finding our way toward a globally interconnected society in which individuals, enterprises, states, and the whole family of peoples and nations could live together peacefully, cooperatively, and with mutual benefit.

A Call for Responsibility

Over the course of the last century, people in many parts of the world have become conscious of their rights as well as of many persistent violations of them. This development is important, but in itself it is not enough. We must now become conscious of the factor without which neither rights nor other values can be effectively safeguarded: our individual and collective responsibilities. We are not likely to grow into a peaceful and cooperative human family unless we become responsible social, economic, political, and cultural actors.

We human beings need more than food, water, and shelter. We need more even than remunerated work, self-esteem and social acceptance. We also need something to live for: an ideal to achieve, a responsibility to accept. Because we are aware of the consequences of our actions, we can and must accept responsibility for them. Such responsibility goes deeper than many of us may think. In today's world all people, no matter where they live and what they do, have become responsible for their actions as:

- private individuals
- citizens
- collaborators in business and the economy
- members of the human community
- persons endowed with mind and consciousness

As individuals, we are responsible for seeking our interests in harmony with the interests and well being of others. We are responsible for condemning and averting any form of killing and brutality; responsible for not bringing more children into the world than we truly need and can support; and responsible for respecting the right to life, development, and equal status and dignity of all the children, women, and men who inhabit the Earth.

As citizens, we are responsible for demanding that our leaders beat swords into ploughshares and relate to other nations peacefully and in a spirit of cooperation; that they recognize the legitimate aspirations of all communities in the human family; and that they do not abuse sovereign powers to manipulate people and the environment for shortsighted and selfish ends.

As collaborators in business and the economy, we are responsible for ensuring that commercial objectives do not center uniquely on profit and growth but include a concern that products and services respond to human needs and demands without harming people and impairing nature; that they do not serve destructive ends and unscrupulous designs; and that they respect the rights of all entrepreneurs and enterprises who compete fairly in the global marketplace.

As members of the human community, it is our responsibility to adopt a culture of non-violence, solidarity, and economic, political, and social equality; to promote mutual understanding and respect among people and nations whether they are like us or different; and to demand that all people everywhere should be empowered to respond to the challenges that face them with the material as well as spiritual resources that are required for this unprecedented task.

And as persons endowed with mind and consciousness, our responsibility is to encourage comprehension and appreciation for the excellence of the human spirit in all its manifestations, and to inspire awe and wonder for a cosmos that brought forth life and consciousness and holds out the possibility of its continued evolution toward ever higher levels of insight, understanding, love, and compassion.

A Call for Planetary Consciousness

In most parts of the world, the real potential of human beings is sadly underdeveloped. The way children are raised depresses their faculties for learning and creativity; the way young people experience the struggle for material survival results in frustration and resentment. In adults this leads to a variety of compensatory, addictive, and compulsive behaviors. The result is

103

the persistence of social and political oppression, economic warfare, cultural intolerance, crime, and disregard for the environment.

Eliminating social and economic ills and frustrations calls for considerable socio-economic development, and that is not possible without better education, information, and communication. These, however, are blocked by the absence of socio-economic development, so that a vicious cycle is produced: underdevelopment creates frustration, and frustration, giving rise to defective behaviors, blocks development. This cycle must be broken at its point of greatest flexibility—the development of the spirit and consciousness of human beings. Achieving this objective does not pre-empt the need for socio-economic development with all its financial and technical resources, but calls for a parallel mission in the spiritual field. Unless people's spirit and consciousness evolve to the planetary dimension, the processes that stress both society and nature will intensify and create a shock wave that could jeopardize the entire transition towards a peaceful and cooperative global society. This would be a setback for humanity and a danger for everyone. Evolving human spirit and consciousness is the first vital cause shared by the whole of the human family.

Planetary consciousness is knowing, as well as feeling, the vital interdependence and essential oneness of humankind. It is the conscious adoption of the ethic and the ethos that this entails. Its evolution is the basic imperative of human survival on this planet.

Adopted by the Club of Budapest on October 26, 1996.

༁

THE CLUB OF BUDAPEST'S

Statements on War and Violence

On Violence

The 11th of September suicide attack on New York's World Trade Center and Washington's Pentagon was an offense against all of human life and every civilization. We condemn this act of terrorism and call on ethical and peace-loving people the world over to join together to put an end to terrorism and violence in all its forms. There is no solution to the world's problems by killing innocent people and destroying their workplaces and habitations.

If we are to succeed in eradicating violence and terrorism, we must act wisely. Violence and terrorism will not be vanquished by retaliation. The ultimate roots of violence lie deeper than the fanatic commitment of terrorists and the religious claims of fundamentalists. Killing one group of terrorists will not solve the problem; as long as the roots are there, others will grow in their place.

The terror that surfaces in today's world is a symptom of longstanding and deep-seated frustrations, resentment, and perceived injustice. We of the Club of Budapest are committed to search for the causes of these hate- and violence-provoking factors and to suggest peaceful and effective ways they can be overcome. Until and unless the root causes are eliminated there will not be peace in the world, only an uncertain interlude between acts of terrorism and larger-scale hostilities. When people are frustrated, harbor hate and the desire for revenge, they cannot relate to each other in a spirit of peace and cooperation. Whether the cause is the wounded ego of a person or the wounded self-respect of a people, and whether it is the wish for personal revenge or a holy war for the defense of a faith, the result is violence, death, and catastrophe. Attaining peace in people's hearts is a precondition for attaining peace in the world.

The Club of Budapest maintains that the wise response to violence and terrorism is to help people to be at peace with themselves and their fellow humans near and far. Promoting solidarity and cooperation in the shared cause of fairness and justice is the only feasible path to lasting peace on Earth.

Adopted by the Club of Budapest on September 15, 2001.

On War

War is a uniquely human phenomenon: no other species kills massively its own kind. Such killing was never justified, but it had a marginal warrant at a time when war was waged among neighboring groups for the acquisition of territory with natural and human resources and could be limited to the territories and the warriors of the protagonists. At a time when resources are not limited to defined territories and hostilities cannot be contained, war is neither politically nor economically justified. Given that modern warfare kills innocent civilians, inflicts serious damage on the life-supporting environment, and may escalate to a global conflagration, waging war is a crime against all of humanity. It needs to be recognized as such. No nation-state should have the legitimate right to declare war on any other nation-state.

The stockpiling of weapons of mass destruction is not a warrant for one nation-state to wage war on another. Weapons of mass destruction—whether they are nuclear, chemical, biological, or conventional—are a threat to human life and habitat by whoever possesses them. They are not tolerable in the hands of any state, whether it is large or small, rich or poor, and headed by a dictator or by an elected politician. Such weapons need to be eliminated from the arsenals of every single state. But this task does not call for waging war and is not the self-declared prerogative of any government but the responsibility of the global community of all peoples and states.

There will be no lasting peace on earth until weapons of mass destruction themselves are destroyed, their production and stockpiling proscribed, and strategies calling for their use replaced by strategies of dialogue, negotiation and, if necessary, internationally agreed economic and political sanctions. Potential aggressors and terrorists must be stopped, but war is not the way to stop them. Fighting violence with violence is to act on the principle of an eye for an eye and a tooth for a tooth, and this will end up making everyone blind and toothless.

The time has come for the world community to recognize that war, far from being an instrument for the elimination of terrorists and aggressors, is itself an act of aggression that threatens human life, and the integrity of the environment on which human life, and all life on earth, vitally depends.

Adopted by the Club of Budapest on February 9, 2003

APPENDICES

 ✌

THE GOI PEACE FOUNDATION'S

Declaration for All Life on Earth

Preamble

The Earth is an evolving living entity. Every form of life on earth is an important part of this living entity. Accordingly, we, as individual human beings, must cultivate the awareness that we are all members of a global community of life and that we share a common mission and responsibility for the future of our planet.

Every one of us has a role to play in the evolution of our planet, and to achieve world peace each of us must live up to our responsibilities and obligations. Up to the present time, few people on earth have been fully satisfied with life. We have faced conflicts all over the world in competition for limited resources and land. This has had a devastating effect on the global environment.

As we enter the new millennium, more than anything else, the realization of world peace depends on an awakening of consciousness on the part of each individual member of the human race. Today, it is imperative that every human being bears the responsibility of building peace and harmony in his or her heart. We all have this common mission that we must fulfill. World peace will be achieved when every member of humanity becomes aware of this common mission—when we all join together for our common purpose.

Until now, in terms of power, wealth, fame, knowledge, technology and education, humanity has been divided between individuals, nations and organizations that have possession and those that do not. There have also been distinctions between the givers and the receivers, the helpers and the helped.

We hereby declare our commitment to transcend all these dualities and distinctions with a totally new concept, which will serve as our foundation as we set out to build a peaceful world.

General Principles

In the new era, humanity shall advance toward a world of harmony, that is, a world in which every individual and every nation can freely express their individual qualities, while living in harmony with one another and with all life on earth. To realize this vision, we set forth the following guiding principles:

1. Reverence for life

We shall create a world based on love and harmony in which all forms of life are respected.

2. Respect for all differences

We shall create a world in which all different races, ethnic groups, religions, cultures, traditions and customs are respected. The world must be a place free from discrimination or confrontation, socially, physically and spiritually—a place where diversity is appreciated and enjoyed.

3. Gratitude for and coexistence with all of nature

We shall create a world in which each person is aware that we are enabled to live through the blessings of nature, and all people live in harmony with nature, showing gratitude for all animal, plant and other forms of life.

4. Harmony between the spiritual and material

We shall create a world based on the harmonious balance of material and spiritual civilization. We must break away from our overemphasis on the material to allow a healthy spirituality to blossom among humanity. We must build a world where not only material abundance but also spiritual riches are valued.

Practice

We shall put these principles into practice guided by the following:

As individuals

We must move beyond an era in which authority and responsibility rest in nation states, ethnic groups and religions to one in which the individual is paramount. We envision an "Age of the Individual"—not in the sense of egoism, but an age in which every individual is ready to accept responsibility and to carry out his or her mission as an independent member of the human race.

Each of us shall carry out our greatest mission to bring love, harmony and gratitude into our own heart, and in so doing, bring harmony to the world at large.

In our specialized fields

We shall build a system of cooperation in which wisdom is gathered together to derive the most from technical knowledge, skills and ability in various fields, such as education, science, culture and the arts, as well as religion, philosophy, politics and economics.

As the young generation

In the 20th century, parents, teachers and society were the educators of children, and the children were always in the position of being taught. In the 21st century, adults shall learn from the wonderful qualities of children, such as their purity, innocence, radiance, wisdom and intuition, to inspire and uplift one another. The young generation shall play a leading role in the creation of peace for a bright future.

May Peace Prevail on Earth

APPENDICES

꒜

A Short Introduction to the Scientific Worldview of the 21st Century

ERVIN LASZLO

There can be no question that science is a major force shaping the world. But most people confuse science with its technological applications. Atomic power, intercontinental and space travel, miracle drugs and instant communication are technological spinoffs of science, and they do shape the world in which we live. But science shapes the world in ways that are more subtle and at the same time more fundamental. Science is more than technology: it is also meaning and knowledge—at its best, it offers genuine insight into the nature of things. These insights shape the vision we have of ourselves, of society and of nature. Science influences our perceptions, colors our feelings, and impacts on our assessment of human worth and social merit. And the insights that are now emerging are of particular relevance to the contemporary world—and to our own lives and our future.

A new view of the world is emerging among cutting-edge physicists, biologists and psychologists. But apart from this select few, most people cling to an obsolete picture of scientific methods and goals (indeed, most readers will be unfamiliar with much of the research and theories presented in this appendix). Science, they believe, produces an abstract and dehumanized picture of the world reduced to numbers and formulas. It follows that the universe is a soulless mechanism, and life in it a random accident. Moreover, the characteristic feature of living organisms result from a succession of accidental events in the history of evolution on Earth, and our own body and mind are the products of a fortuitous combination of the genes with which we happen to be born. These widely-held views of cosmos, life and mind are rapidly being supplanted by new discoveries.*

What does the emerging scientific world view have to do with you, a global citizen confronting the challenges of responsible thinking and acting in the pragmatic context of an exploited and crisis-prone planet? More, perhaps, than you may think. The world view coming from the frontiers of the sciences lends fresh significance to your existence. You may be an inhabitant of a small planet in a smallish solar system at the edge of a galaxy, but with your conscious mind you are one of the truly evolved manifestations of the great cosmic trend that brought forth galaxies, stars and planets in space and time, as well as life and mind of ever greater complexity and sophistication on the surface of this sun-bathed planet.

This insight should deepen your commitment to peace and sustainability and reinforce your sense of responsibility. Because it is up to you, a living being endowed with reason and consciousness, to ensure that evolution on this planet does not lead to a dead end; that it continues the grand adventure of our species by creating a world of coherence, cooperation and coevolution.

A New Concept of Matter and Space

The shift in science's view of the world has altered our most fundamental conceptions of matter and space. Until relatively

---

* For further details see, Ervin Laszlo, *The Whispering Pond*, Element Books, 1996, and Ervin Laszlo, *The Connectivity Hypothesis*, State University of New York Press, 2003.

recently, the commonly-held Western view had been that matter and space coexist: they are the ultimate furnishings of reality. Matter occupies space and moves about in it, and space serves as a backdrop or container. This classical concept was radically revised, both in Einstein's relativistic universe, where space/time is an integrated four-dimensional manifold, and also in the new and strange world of quantum physics. Now it is being rethought again.

In light of what scientists are beginning to learn about the nature of the quantum vacuum, the energy sea that underlies all of space and time, it is no longer warranted to view matter as primary and space as secondary. It is to space—or rather, to the cosmically extended "zero-point field" of the quantum vacuum—that we must grant primacy.

The reason for the shift from matter to energy as the primary reality lies in the discovery that, notwithstanding its name, the quantum vacuum is not empty space (a "vacuum"), but filled space: a plenum. It is the locus of the zero-point field, so named because the energies of this field persist even when all other energies vanish—at the zero point.

In itself, this vast field is not electromagnetic, gravitational or nuclear. Instead, it is the source of the known electromagnetic, gravitational and nuclear forces and fields. It is also the origin of the matter particles themselves. By stimulating the zero-point field of the vacuum with sufficient energy, a particular region of it is "kicked" from the state of negative energy into the state of positive energy. This makes for "pair-creation": out of the vacuum emerges a positive energy (real) particle, with its twin, a negative energy (virtual) particle, remaining inside the vacuum.

The energy density of the zero-point field is almost inconceivable. According to physicist John Wheeler of Princeton University, the matter-equivalent of its energy density (that is the amount of matter that would be required to bring together this much energy) is 10^{94} gram/cm^3. But a density of 10 (to the 94th power) calculates to an exponentially greater amount of energy/matter than is calculated to exist in the entire universe!

It is fortunate indeed that the energies of the vacuum are "virtual". Otherwise, given that energy is equivalent to mass and mass exerts gravitation, the superdense universe would instantly collapse to a size smaller than the head of a pin.

In light of these discoveries, a radical new hypothesis is emerging: the material universe is not a solidification of vacuum energies, but a thinning of them—a one-hundred and eighty degree shift from the idea that matter is dense, autonomous, and moving through passive and empty space.

The matter that furnishes the universe we inhabit emerged when the quantum vacuum became destabilized in the cosmic explosion known as the Big Bang. The enormous energies liberated by it brought forth pairs of particles (particles-antiparticles) from the vacuum. Those that did not annihilate each other make up the matter that now furnishes our bodies, our planet, our solar system, and the rest of the universe.

The particles of matter that survived those first milliseconds in the life of the universe are still in constant, if subtle, interaction with the virtual energy field from which they emerged. Bold new theories—by Harold Puthoff of the University of Texas at Austin; Bernhard Haisch and Alfonso Rueda, both of the University of California at Berkeley; among others—suggest that all basic characteristics of matter (mass, gravitation and inertia) are products of the interaction of charged particles with the zero-point field.

The work of a group of Russian physicists is of particular significance. According to the "torsion-field theory of the physical vacuum" developed by Anatoly Akimov and G.I. Shipov of the University of Moscow along with other collaborators, all objects, from quanta to galaxies, create vortices in the vacuum—spins in the cosmic ether. These torsion waves travel at one billion times the speed of light and they endure: they persist even in the absence of the objects that generated them.

The existence of "torsion-wave phantoms" has been confirmed in the experiments of Vladimir Poponin and his team at the Institute of Biochemical Physics of the Russian Academy of Sciences. Poponin, who has since repeated the experiments at the Heartmath Institute in the U.S., placed a sample of a DNA molecule into a temperature-controlled chamber and subjected it to a laser beam. He found that the electromagnetic field around the chamber exhibits a specific structure, more or less as expected. But he also found that this structure persists long after the DNA itself has been removed from the laser-irradiated chamber; the DNA's imprint in the field continues to be present even after the DNA is no longer there. Poponin and his collaborators concluded that the experiment shows that a new field structure has been triggered in the physical vacuum. The phantom effect appears to be a manifestation of a hitherto overlooked substructure in the energy sea that pervades the universe.

Emerging Insights into the Nature of Life and Mind

Living organisms are also embedded in the universe's underlying energy field, and they, too, are affected by it. Life evolves, as does the universe itself, in a "sacred dance" with the underlying cosmic energy field. This means that living organisms are not skin-enclosed entities, and the living world is not the harsh domain envisaged by Darwin, where each struggles against all, with every species, every organism and every gene competing for advantage against every other.

Advances in theoretical physics have profound implications for our understanding of human consciousness. After all, our brains—along with our bodies and everything else in the universe—must be embedded in this vast and complex web of relations. We are not isolated entities. The information that reaches our brain is not limited to our own body and to organisms and things in our immediate vicinity. It is also not limited to the visible spectrum of electromagnetic waves and the audible spectrum of sonic waves; the flow of information available to us consists of all the waves of the zero-point field. According to this model, traffic between our brain and the rest of the world is constant and flows in both directions. Everything that goes on in our mind leaves its wave-traces in the embedding cosmic field, and everything in that field can be "read out" again by the brain—as long as this information is not repressed by our everyday consciousness.

Mathematician John von Neumann calculated that the amount of information accumulated during an average life-span is about 2.8×10^{20} "bits". This is a staggering amount. How could the human brain, enclosed in a small and finite cranium, manage this feat? The answer is that it is not the brain itself that stores the experiences that make up long-term memory; the brain only accesses this information. Storage itself is extra-somatic: it is in the subtle but real cosmic field in which the organism is embedded.

In light of the evidence uncovered at the leading edge of contemporary consciousness research, psychologist Carl Jung's insight is vindicated. In addition to our individual consciousness, there is also a collective human consciousness—even a cosmic consciousness. These wider spheres of consciousness are rooted in the subtle wave-patterns of the quantum vacuum; in the universe's encompassing and ever-present information field.

In Summary

In the emerging world view of the sciences, there is no categorical divide between the physical world, the living world, and the world of mind and consciousness. Life and mind are consistent elements within an overall process of great complexity, yet harmonious design. Space and time are united as the dynamic background of the observable universe; matter is vanishing as a fundamental feature of reality, retreating before energy; and continuous fields are replacing discrete particles as the basic elements of an energy-bathed universe. The cosmos is a seamless whole, evolving over eons of time and producing conditions where life can emerge. The biosphere is born within the womb of the universe, and mind and consciousness are born in the womb of the biosphere. Our body is part of the biosphere and it resonates with the web of life on this planet. And our mind is part of our body, in touch with other minds as well as the biosphere.

Thousands of years ago, the Chinese sage Chuang Tzu wrote, "Heaven, Earth and I are living together, and all things and I form an inseparable unity." In their latest developments, the new sciences are rediscovering and reconfirming such intuitions. They find fresh and dependable answers to ecologist Gregory Bateson's oft-cited question, "What pattern connects the crab to the lobster and the orchid to the primrose and all four of them to me? And me to you?" There is such a pattern: it is in the cosmic information field that connects you and me, and all things in the universe. Williams James was right: We are like islands in the sea—separate on the surface but connected in the deep.

A Concise Guide to
Further Reading

❧

COMPILED BY DAVID WOOLFSON

The Club of Budapest Canada

Basic Orientation

Dalai Lama, H.H. *Ethics for the New Millennium.* Riverhead Books 2001.

Gorbachev, Mikhail. *On My Country and the World.* Columbia University Press 1999.

Hammond, Allen. *Which World: Scenarios for the 21st Century: Global Destinies, Regional Choices.* Shearwater Books 2000.

Laszlo, Ervin. *Macroshift: Navigating the Transformation to a Sustainable World.* Berret-Koehler 2001.

Muller, Robert and Douglas Roche. *Safe Passage into the Twenty-First Century.* Continuum Pub Group 1995.

Strong, Maurice. *Where on Earth Are We Going?* Texere 2001.

World Commission on Environment and Development. *Our Common Future.* Oxford University Press 1987.

Facts about the State of the World

United Nations Development Program. *Human Development Report 2002: Deepening Democracy in a Fragmented World.* Oxford University Press 2002.

United Nations Environment Program. *Global Environment Outlook 3: United Nations Environment Programme (Global Environment Outlook Series).* Earthscan Publications Ltd. 2002.

Worldwatch Institute (Editor). *State of the World 2003.* W.W. Norton & Company 2003.

Worldwatch Institute (Editor). *Vital Signs 2002: Consumers Pressure Businesses to Go Green.* W.W. Norton & Company 2002.

Perspectives on the Future

Daly, Herman. *For the Common Good: Redirecting the Economy toward Community, the Environment and a Sustainable Future.* Beacon Press 1994.

Hertsgaard, Mark. *Earth Odyssey: Around the World in Search of Our Environmental Future.* Broadway Books 1999.

Homer-Dixon, Thomas. *The Ingenuity Gap.* Alfred A. Knopf 2000.

Laszlo, Ervin. *The Choice: Evolution or Extinction?: A Thinking Person's Guide to Global Issues.* J.P. Tarcher 1994.

Linden, Eugene. *The Future in Plain Sight.* Penguin Putnam Inc. 2002.

Mayor, Federico and Jerome Bind. *The World Ahead: Our Future in the Making.* Zed Books 2001.

Rischard, Jeanfrancois. *High Noon 20 Global Problems, 20 Years to Solve Them.* Basic Books 2003.

Wilson, Edward O. *The Future of Life.* Alfred A. Knopf 2002.

Issues of Ecological Sustainability

Benyus, Janine M. *Biomimicry: Innovation Inspired by Nature.* William Morrow & Co. 1998.

Brown, Lester. *Eco-Economy: Building a New Economy for the Environmental Age.* W. W. Norton & Company 2001.

Copley, Anthony and George Paxton. *Gandhi and the Contemporary World.* The Indo-British Historical Society 1997.

Hartmann, Thom, *The Prophet's Way: Touching the Power of Life.* Three Rivers Press 1997.

Hawken, Paul. *The Ecology of Commerce.* Harper Collins 1994.

Hawken, Paul, A. Lovins, and L. Hunter. *Natural Capitalism: Creating the Next Industrial Revolution.* Little Brown & Company 1999.

Henderson, Hazel. *Building a Win-Win World: Life Beyond Global Economic Welfare.* Berrett-Koehler 1996.

Henderson, Hazel. *Beyond Globalization: Shaping a Sustainable Global Economy.* Kumarian Press 1999.

Nattrass, Brian and Mary Altomare. *The Natural Step for Business: Wealth, Ecology and the Evolutionary Corporation (Conscientious Commerce).* New Society Publishers 1999.

Approaches to Peace and Human Security

Ackerman, Peter and Jack Duvall. *A Force More Powerful: A Century of Nonviolent Conflict.* St. Martin's Press 2001.

Dorn, A. Walter (Editor). *World Order for a New Millennium: Political, Cultural and Spiritual Approaches to Building Peace.* Palgrave 1999.

Ferencz, Benjamin. *Planethood: The Key to Your Future.* Love Line Books 1991.

Herzog, Roman. *Preventing the Clash of Civilizations: A Peace Strategy for the Twenty-First Century.* Palgrave 1999.

Hunt, Scott A. *The Future of Peace: On the Front Lines with the World's Great Peacemakers.* Harper San Francisco 2002.

Lederach, John Paul. *Building Peace: Sustainable Reconciliation in Divided Societies.* United States Institute of Peace 1997.

Rotblat, Joseph, Maxwell Bruce, and Tom Milne, (Editors). *Ending War: The Force of Reason*. Palgrave 1999.

Schell, Jonathan. *The Fate of the Earth: The Abolition*. Stanford University Press 2000.

Schell, Jonathan. *The Unconquerable World: Power, Nonviolence, and the Will of the People*. Metropolitan Books 2003.

Thomas, Caroline. *Global Governance, Development and Human Security*. Stylus Publishers LLC. 2001.

Paths to Global Transformation

Berry, Thomas. *The Great Work: Our Way Into the Future*. Harmony Books 2000.

Elgin, Duane. *Promise Ahead: A Vision of Hope and Action for Humanity's Future*. William Morrow & Co. 2000.

Elgin Duane. *Voluntary Simplicity*. William Morrow & Co. 1993.

Goodall, Jane. *Reason for Hope: A Spiritual Journey*. Warner Books 2000.

Harman, Willis. *Global Mind Change*. Berrett-Koehler 1998.

Hock, Dee. *Birth of the Chaordic Age*. Berrett-Koehler 1999.

Hubbard, Barbara Marx. *Conscious Evolution: Awakening the Power of our Societal Potential*. New World Library 1997.

Korten, David C. *The Post-Corporate World*. Berrett-Koehler 1999.

Quinn, Daniel. *Beyond Civilization: Humanity's Next Great Adventure*. Three Rivers Press 2000.

Ray, Paul and Sherry Ruth Anderson. *The Cultural Creatives: How 50 Million People Are Changing the World*. Harmony Books 2001.

Russell, Peter. *The Global Brain Awakens*. Element 2000.

Zohar, Danah and Ian Marshall. *The Quantum Society: Mind, Physics, and a New Social Vision*. Quill 1995.

BIOGRAPHIES

〜

Ervin Laszlo

Ervin Laszlo is Founder and President of The Club of Budapest, Founder and Director of the General Evolution Research Group, Administrator of the Interdisciplinary University of Paris, Fellow of the World Academy of Arts and Sciences, Member of the International Academy of Philosophy of Science, Senator of the International Medici Academy, and Editor of the international periodical *World Futures: The Journal of General Evolution*. Laszlo is the author or co-author of forty-five books translated into as many as twenty languages, and the editor of another twenty-nine volumes including a four-volume encyclopedia.

Considered the foremost exponent of systems philosophy and general evolution theory, Laszlo's recent research centers on the development of an integral science of quantum, cosmos, life, and consciousness. In addition to his theoretical work,

Laszlo is noted for his work in the futures and management fields. He has a PhD from the Sorbonne and is the recipient of four honorary PhD's (from the United States, Canada, Finland, and Hungary), the Goi Peace Prize of Japan, and other distinctions. Formerly Professor of Philosophy, Systems Science, and Futures Studies in various universities in the U.S., Europe and the Far East, Laszlo lectures worldwide, and during 2003/2004 holds a visiting Professorship at the University of Stuttgart, Germany.

Presently Laszlo lives in a four-hundred year-old converted farmhouse in Tuscany with his Finnish-born wife Carita. His sons Christopher and Alexander, who live with their families in the United States, follow in his footsteps, the former in the sustainability and ethical management consulting field and the latter in the academic domain where together with his wife Kathia he combines evolutionary theory with evolutionary community counseling.

56040 Montescudaio (Pisa)
Italy
Fax: +39-0586-650395
E-mail: laszlo@etrurianet.it

BIOGRAPHIES

Masami Saionji

Masami Saionji is Chairperson of The Goi Peace Foundation and The World Peace Prayer Society. She is also an honorary member of The Club of Budapest. A descendant of the Royal Ryukyu Family of Okinawa, she continues the work of her adoptive father, Masahisa Goi, who initiated a movement for world peace through the universal prayer "May Peace Prevail on Earth." As a spiritual leader, respected both in Japan and internationally, she has touched thousands of people's lives through her guidance and inspiration.

Ms. Saionji is the author of seventeen books, four of which have been published in English and other languages: *The Golden Key to Happiness, Infinite Happiness, You Are the Universe,* and *The Earth Healer's Handbook.*

She travels extensively on speaking tours, and has led peace ceremonies in many countries as well as at the United Nations and other international organizations. She and her husband, Hiroo Saionji live in Tokyo and have three daughters.

The Goi Peace Foundation
1-4-5- Hirakawacho
Chiyoda-ky, Tokyo 102-0093
Japan
Email: info@goipeace.or.jp
http://www.goipeace.or.jp

The World Peace Prayer Society
at the World Peace Sanctuary
26 Benton Road
Wassaic, NY 12592 USA
Email: info@worldpeace.org
http://www.worldpeace.org

ॐ THE CLUB OF BUDAPEST
OF NORTH AMERICA

This book is co-published by The Club of Budapest of North America, an international non-profit (501-c-3) organization created to enhance the Club of Budapest's mission in North America, in association with the Club of Budapest USA, the Club of Budapest Canada, and the Club of Budapest Mexico.

The Club of Budapest is an international non-profit organization dedicated to advancing a new thinking and a new ethic that better prepares us to meet the challenges and issues of the 21st century. Founded in 1993 by Professor Ervin Laszlo, the Club is dedicated to promoting the new thinking and acting we need to move toward a peaceful and sustainable world.

For additional information on bulk discounts of this book or other information on the activities and membership opportunities for the Club of Budapest of North America please contact the following:

Carl Zaiss
Executive Director
The Club of Budapest of North America
6001 Pocol Drive
Clifton, VA 20124
703-631-1427 phone
703-631-0427 fax
carl@carlzaiss.com

For bookseller purchases please contact the following:

Kenzi Sugihara
President
SelectBooks, Inc.
One Union Square West
Suite 909
New York, NY 10003
212-206-1997 phone
212-206-3815 fax
ks.selectbooks@ix.netcom.com